Endors

M000237998

Biblical and purposeful. These two words say so much. God's word is one hundred per cent purposeful. Having spent over 40 years of my life giving financial advice and helping many make financial decisions, I believe that a Biblical approach to managing the financial resources entrusted to us by our Lord is the only rational approach to money and money management. Mike and Eric have precisely identified what plagues so many believers from achieving that aim. This book will steer you away from "Default Financial Planning" and give you clarity on your stewardship journey. I recommend this book without reservation.

—Ron Blue, Founder or co-founder of Ronald Blue Trust,
National Christian Foundation,
Kingdom Advisors, and The Ron Blue Institute for
Financial Planning.

Mike and Eric share a passion to seek the financial and spiritual good of their clients. Their rare synthesis of wisdom for stewarding money and navigating life is distilled in this book. Reading these pages will help you to take better care of your money and of your soul.

—Colin S. Smith, Senior Pastor, The Orchard
Founder and Bible Teacher, Open the Bible

In this book, Mike and Eric masterfully weave together biblical truths about money with practical wisdom on financial planning. Using real-life stories from their decades of experience, they help readers find true financial contentment through reminders that our resources, our work, and our money are all gifts from God. The authors' advice on spending, saving, investing, and retirement is sage, distilled from Scripture, and applicable to all who are exploring a Biblical view of money.

—D. Michael Lindsay, President, Taylor University

Beyond bigger barns to a better purpose! *Thinking Biblically and Purposefully About Your Wealth* will lead you to not only want to do better with your wealth but be equipped to do so for the glory of God.

—Dr. Josh Moody, Senior Pastor,
College Church in Wheaton
President, God Centered Life Ministries

Mike and Eric clearly and succinctly explain the need for a biblical understanding of money in all areas of personal finance. This book will simultaneously challenge and encourage you towards contentment, generosity, and stewardship.

—Rob West, CEO, Kingdom Advisors
Host, Nationally Syndicated Radio Program *MoneyWise*

Money management is surprisingly important to God, and I know of no one better to explain His financial principles than Eric and Mike. Unlike most wealth managers, these men have a deep and biblical understanding of true financial success. Their book will bless you with clear and strategic guidance that will steer you away from money's pitfalls and guide you into the significance and joy that wealth was meant to produce.

—Jeff Griffin, Senior Pastor, The Compass Church

Thinking Biblically &

Purposefully about Your

WEALTH

MICHAEL MCKEVITT

& ERIC FRECKMAN

FREILING
PUBLISHING

Copyright © 2022 by Michael McKevitt and Eric Freckman
First Paperback Edition

All rights reserved. No part of this publication may be reproduced,
distributed, or transmitted in any form or by any means, including
photocopying, recording, or other electronic or mechanical methods,
without the prior written permission of the publisher, except in the
case of brief quotations embodied in critical reviews and
certain other noncommercial uses permitted by copyright law.
For permission requests, write to the publisher, addressed
"Attention: Permissions Coordinator," at the address below.

Scriptures are taken from The Holy Bible, English Standard Version. ESV®
Text Edition: 2016. Copyright © 2001 by Crossway Bibles, a publishing
ministry of Good News Publishers.

Some names, businesses, places, events, locales, incidents,
and identifying details inside this book have been changed
to protect the privacy of individuals.

Published by Freiling Publishing, a division of Freiling Agency, LLC.

P.O. Box 1264
Warrenton, VA 20188

www.FreilingPublishing.com

PB ISBN: 978-1-956267-83-9
eBook ISBN: 978-1-956267-84-6

Printed in the United States of America

Dedication

Eric – This book is dedicated to my wife, Jennifer, and our four children: Olivia, Josiah, Cade, and Kaylee. Thank you, Jen, for the love, trust, and support from the beginning. I love you and the life we are building. To my kids – I pray that you would not remember a day when you did not love and follow Jesus. I promise that Jesus is worth it all and I pray you live your life accordingly. I love being your dad.

Mike – This book is dedicated to my wife, Whitney, and to our children: Dylan, Cameron, Sadie, and Cora. Thank you, Whitney, for all the love and support you give me, especially in making this book a reality. To our children, my prayer and hope is that you will follow the Lord wholeheartedly and joyfully rest in God's love for you and His plan for your life.

Soli Deo Gloria

Contents

Introduction

HOW MUCH IS enough? Our culture screams at us to keep hustling, working, and investing to have more, but does it ever talk about the cost of living this way? It's time to acknowledge that this is a cycle that doesn't end. Throughout the following pages, you will learn how we've helped our clients find a better way with their finances.

If you're a Christian, you have God's word to show you the better way. Author and financial services entrepreneur Ron Blue has said that all good financial advice is biblical. This comes not only from a belief that all truth is God's truth, but also from the observation that the actual financial wisdom found in the Bible forms the guiding principles found in any good financial advice today.

We wholeheartedly agree, and have seen the impact this truth can have through our work in a financial planning practice for a combined total of over 35 years. We know these principles can lead to improved financial decision making, but also, more importantly, increased contentment in all areas of life. There is a better way.

Let's start with James and Catherine. They are long-time clients who aggressively saved and invested since their first jobs. For quite a while they were on cruise control—making prudent financial decisions but not necessarily putting a lot of thought into what they were working toward. As the dollars started to add up, so did the stress and lack of joy. It was during this time that we noticed the change in their attitudes. We discussed questions like: do you want to do this for another twenty years? Would you do something different if money was not an issue? What if climbing the corporate ladder was causing more harm than good?

This started a conversation that lasted months as we helped them define "enough." To their surprise, they really did not need to save much more money. They still needed to earn income to support their lifestyle, but no longer need to save a big portion of their income. James and Catherine shifted their mindset from asset maximization to living a more balanced life. They began this process by taking jobs that were less demanding on their time.

> Our desire is for you to see the freedom that contentment offers.

They traded striving to get more for contentment in what they currently had. There had always been another dollar to earn, another sale to make, or another deal to close. They finally said "enough" and made the choice to go against the grain. They began to prioritize time with their high-school-aged kids and got involved with causes they cared about. They cared less about having additional dollars in their investment accounts. With these changes, joy returned.

This is why we do the work that we do. Most everyone has heard some version of, "If money is where you find your happiness, you'll always be poor," but we can walk into the trap of looking to money for happiness without even noticing. Our desire for you is to see the freedom that contentment offers.

When investing for the first time, watching your investments can be exciting. People will often find a new interest in what the stock market is doing and log in repeatedly to their account to watch the balance change—perhaps out of anticipation for what they might have gained, or perhaps out of nervousness for what they might have lost. Over time, this obsessive level of attention fades (which it should—investing should be boring! More on this later), yet often a hope the investment will strike it big remains. 1 Timothy 6:6 says, "Godliness with contentment is great gain." There are many great books about godliness,* but our focus will be on the contentment aspect. While great gains seem to be the purpose of our financial lives, where does contentment fit in? How does this play out in lives with growing demands from work, families, and the general busyness of life?

We believe that contentment is possible and should play a major role in financial decisions and stewardship. Our aim is to show you how this can be done and how we've seen this play out in the lives of people just like you.

Consider Adam and Sarah. Adam and Sarah did not do much financial planning during their forties and early fifties because it was not a priority. They were comfortable and Sarah was able to stay home to raise their three kids, but they were not intentional about their finances. In their late fifties, the company Adam worked for went public. His stock, which he never paid much attention to, was worth a significant amount of money. The company was also offering more stock to entice Adam to keep working and growing the company. The work was hard and Adam was traveling most weeks, then trying to recover each weekend before he found himself at the airport again Monday

---

* See "For Further Reading" at the end of the book.

morning. Seemingly overnight, Adam and Sarah were faced with questions they had never considered before. Can they afford to retire? Do they even want to retire? What would life look like if they retired? What would they do all day? What do they want to spend the next phase of their life doing?

Adam decided that he wanted to stop working for the newly public company, but he was not sure he wanted to retire completely. In his mind, the windfall he received from the company stock meant that he had reached the pinnacle of his career and he should retire. However, he wasn't ready to be "put out to pasture." He was just ready for the next phase of life and wasn't sure how work would fit into that phase.

During our discussions, Adam realized that he would be leaving a lot of money on the table if he left his job because he would be given more stock the longer he stayed. This brought up more questions about how much is "enough." Would Adam be a better steward if he continued to work, received the stock, and then gave it to charitable organizations he supported? These discussions involved more money than Adam had ever thought possible and it was hard for him to understand what this meant for him.

Eventually Adam decided to work a bit longer and then leave his job and take time to figure out his next steps. After a few months of not working, he joined a smaller company in a similar industry. It was an opportunity that increased his impact on the people he worked with and decreased his travel. Having spent several months contemplating their future and finances, Adam and Sarah now felt freedom—freedom to make choices based on what they valued and not on what was typical for those who suddenly find themselves with unexpected resources.

James and Catherine and Adam and Sarah did not appear to have much in common, but they were asking the same questions about finding contentment and how much is "enough." They desired the "great gain" that comes from godliness with contentment, but were not sure what it looked like in a world where more is always better and contentment is elusive. We desire to provide the framework and practical strategies for people like them to answer these questions. It is not straightforward or quick. It is much easier to simply keep working and maximizing dollars because that is what everyone else is doing (this is what we call Default Financial Planning and we'll cover it in Chapter 2). Doing something different and against the flow of culture can be hard, but the potential rewards can be worth the risk.

> We want to offer you encouragement to reject the endless pursuit of more and instead pursue contentment and stewardship in your financial life.

The questions each couple asked might have been somewhat similar, but the life application was much different. This is the unique facet of financial advice. The answers to these questions, even for people that have the same biblical convictions, can be different based on their circumstances and what God is doing in their life.

The world is full of financial how-to books. We don't think that is what you need, and it is not what we're writing. We want to offer you encouragement to reject the endless pursuit of more and instead pursue contentment and stewardship in your financial life. We believe it can change your life and the lives of those you desire to impact. We've seen it happen.

1

True Contentment

GROWING UP, NORTHERN Wisconsin, with seemingly endless snowmobile trails, was a favorite destination for Mike's family in the winter. After getting back from a ride, everything from my jacket to my long johns would be cold and wet so I would hang them in the cabin's furnace room to dry. The cabin was heated by a wood burning stove, located in the furnace room, that kept that room incredibly warm. When it was time for the next ride, the gear was warm and cozy. This is what Puritan author Jeremiah Burroughs described as being made content by an external factor.

However, Burroughs would argue, this is not true contentment. In The Rare Jewel of Christian Contentment, Burroughs describes true contentment as coming from within—like a man's clothes that are warmed by his body heat and not an external source like the furnace room. True contentment comes from our heart and soul. Think of Paul and Silas in the Philippian jail. After the guards beat them with rods, they were thrown into the inner prison of the jail and chained. We would all understand if that day of all days they were upset and spent the night recovering, yet we're told they were found around midnight praying and singing hymns. This is Paul living out what he tells us in Philippians 4:11—he learned to be content, even in prison where it was certainly not coming from anything external.

We've all had the experience of getting a new phone and taking such good care of it... for a few weeks. Pretty soon we treat it the same way we treated our old phone, and we don't think much about the new features we once had to have. The shine wore off surprisingly fast. In our hearts, we know that having more stuff and buying more things will not make us happy for long.

But what is within us that can bring about true contentment? Contemporary author Erik Raymond draws on Burroughs and other great minds throughout Christian history to define contentment as "the inward, gracious, quiet spirit that joyfully rests in God's providence."[1] What brings about true contentment is resting in God's providence—His caring provision for His people—with great joy because of what He has done for us. God graciously teaches us contentment as we grow in our knowledge of Him and how He is working in our lives. But like many aspects of the Christian life, true contentment also takes effort on our part (while God is at work pursuing our sanctification).

This is not what the world around us teaches. Rather, we find ourselves in a world that thrives on discontentment—a world that repeatedly promises us that the latest and greatest widget will bring us happiness.

Our Discontented Culture

The fact that this broken world is built upon false promises that distort God's good gifts should not surprise us—we see pain and heartache all around us. A common theme of the New Testament is that followers of Christ are exiles and sojourners on this earth. This is not our permanent home, and we must remember that in all areas of our lives we live as temporary residents in this broken world. Consider the ways this culture of discontentment creeps into so many aspects of our lives:

Family – Our culture displays discontentment with family in two divergent ways. The first is the view that family holds us back from what we really want to be doing—from living our "best lives." If only we did not have responsibilities like raising kids or caring for aging parents, we could do what makes us happy. On the other hand, and far more prevalent in Christian culture, is the view that family is the center of everything. We seem to think what will make us truly happy is the perfect Christmas card with our well-dressed children in front of the fireplace of our large home with high-end finishes in the right neighborhood where we have the right kind of friends.

Not only are these wrong views of the family, but neither delivers the promised happiness. The world is selling bold-faced lies, two sides of the same coin that always lands with discontentment face up. Disappointment comes when abandoning our families doesn't make our best life a reality or when we end up with an imperfect family, full of disputes, illnesses, poor grades, or foolish behaviors.

Work – One of the first questions we ask when meeting someone new is, "What do you do?" Perhaps we ask it as an easy conversation starter to get to know someone, but perhaps many—if not most—people look to their job for satisfaction, purpose, and meaning in their lives. Who wouldn't want to talk about that? We'll cover this in more detail in our chapter on work, but a culture of discontentment thrives in the vocational aspect of our lives—if we aren't climbing the ladder fast enough, if someone else is getting promoted, if the big deal doesn't go through, if our work is mundane, and the list could go on and on. Our culture tells us to keep going because prestige, approval of others, and financial success await us if we just work harder. In the meantime, those are just more areas in which we grow discontent.

Social – If we go to the right church, we'll make the right kind of friends—the kind of friends that take fun vacations together that we see on Instagram. We choose our friends, unlike our families, so we think if we don't have great relationships, we must be doing it wrong, or something is wrong with us. Why weren't we invited to that concert or to that playdate with other moms in our kid's class? Do you see how the world is selling lies? It takes the God-given gift of friendship and turns it into something to be unhappy with. We assume that we weren't included because we don't have a certain amount of money or live in that neighborhood or have membership in that club. Perhaps you have seen the episode of *Friends* where their different incomes nearly tore the group apart. It's funny because it hits close to home.

Physical – We live in a world that idolizes physical beauty and health. We also live in a country that loves fast food. Has there ever been a clearer equation for discontentment? Think about all the advertisements for gyms, diets, and healthy meals. Think about the filters on your phone's camera and all the apps that make it so easy to adjust the true photo to better fit expectations. The messaging behind all of this is clear: happiness lies in being fit and beautiful. Of course, it doesn't stop there. We also need to belong to the right gym or if we work out at home it needs to be on a Peloton or if we're runners we must have the newest running shoe.

These are just a few examples of ways that our culture takes good gifts from God and turns them into things to be discontent with. We find it so easy to idolize these things and make them ultimate in our lives instead of Christ.

Financial Contentment

Many of these examples have financial discontentment at their core. Perhaps it is a chicken and egg type of situation—does financial discontentment lead to discontentment elsewhere or vice versa? Whichever it is, there is no denying that financial discontentment is a leading source of pain in our culture.

> There is no greater danger to our devotion to Jesus than wealth; instead of our hearts and minds being focused on Jesus they become focused on our bank accounts.

Let's look at our definition of contentment again: the inward, gracious, quiet spirit that joyfully rests in God's providence. How does that definition work when thinking about money? The key will be remembering biblical truths in light of God's providence.

Think first of Matthew 6:24. Jesus had just taught about laying up treasures in heaven rather than on earth when he says, "No one can serve two masters, for either he will hate the one and love the other, or he will be devoted to the one and despise the other. You cannot serve God and money." This is the first principle to keep in mind: we cannot allow money to become our master. Jesus has called us to abandon all things that threaten our devotion to Him. There is no greater danger to our devotion to Jesus than wealth. The Bible talks more about money than about heaven. Our hearts are prone to wander; instead of our hearts and minds being focused on Jesus they become focused on our bank accounts.

The second biblical truth we must remember is from Ecclesiastes 5:10: "He who loves money will not be satisfied with money." God's caring provision for us includes teaching us that we will never find satisfaction in money and warning us to not allow it to take priority in our lives. The Bible does not teach that money itself is evil, but rather that the *love* of money is evil. Money is simply a tool, but how we use that tool reveals our hearts. How we use it can be good or bad (and often somewhere in between). We'll dive deeper into that idea in the coming pages, but first let's briefly reflect on how we, as believers, are doing when it comes to being content in our finances.

Reflect on Christian culture in this country. Does your handling of personal finances look any different from the rest of society? What about your church? Your circle of friends? Many people are giving to charity, but is the giving sacrificial? Think about how money is spent—are we being wise stewards of what we've been entrusted with? Think about how we accumulate wealth—do we know how much is enough? Are we content because we have the things we want (the external sources we started the chapter with) or are we content because of what is inside of us (a joyful spirit resting and trusting in God)?

Broadly speaking, we fail to see a significant difference between the world and most Christians when it comes to dealing with money. We see many families handling finances by default—doing the same things with our money that we see everyone else doing because we think we should. We call this Default Financial Planning and we will look at it next in our consideration of contentment and stewardship. The goal is to be sojourners living *in* this world but not *like* this world, so that our freedom and contentment can shine for Christ in a world consumed by fear and greed.

2

Default Financial Planning

SEVERAL YEARS AGO, there was a well-known bank that had a series of memorable commercials in which people would carry around large orange dollar amounts that were "their number." In one of these commercials a man was trimming a hedge and his neighbor came walking down the sidewalk holding his number. The camera pans over and we now see that the man who is trimming his hedge has a number too: "$Gazillion." The neighbor asked, "How do you plan for that?" and the reply was, "I just throw money at it and hope something good happens." The point was clear: you can't just hope for the best—you need a plan to help get you where you want to go.

> Default Financial Planning is when we do things with our money that we see other people doing, just because we think that's what we're supposed to do.

Does that commercial sting a little? Can you identify with the man who is hoping something good will just happen with the money that he saves from time to time? While the commercial succeeded in being memorable (can you remember the people carrying around their numbers?), it didn't revolutionize how people handle their money. There continues to be a lack of thoughtfulness and planning around finances. The current approach seems to be more like that of a Nike commercial: "Just do it." Don't have a plan. Don't even think about it too much. Just do what you think you're supposed to do—what everyone else is doing. We see it so often that we've come up with a term for it: Default Financial Planning. Default Financial Planning is when we do things with our money that we see other people doing, just because we think that's what we're supposed to do. If it works for everyone else, it must be the best thing for me as well, right? The cues we get on how to handle our finances come from several different sources and we'll look at each of them. We just saw how this world thrives on discontentment and you'll see that pattern continue.

Sources of Influence

Perhaps there is no greater source of pressure in our financial lives than the workplace. In our jobs, we can compare ourselves to others based on some knowledge of whether the comparison is fair or not. We know where everyone stands in the hierarchy. It is also the place where we are most "on display"—the clothes we wear, the car we drive, weekend plans, vacation plans…everyone sees everyone and it's all too easy to start making choices based on comparisons.

When the sales team has a good quarter and one of them shows up the next week with a new Tesla, suddenly and subtly others begin to question the car they drive and associate a good quarter with a new purchase. It doesn't matter if they might have been saving for months to pay for it with cash or if it was leased or financed. Discontentment still creeps in. The same can be said of raises and promotions. We take cues from our coworkers for how we are to spend this new money. It can be even easier in large companies because salary ranges for different levels of seniority are often widely known.

The pressure from the workplace extends beyond your lifestyle—it also impacts how you invest. It's commonplace to talk around the water cooler about successful trades (but notice the silence on the trades that didn't turn out well). This can make you feel like you're missing out on easy money. Pretty soon you have a newfound interest in bitcoin, meme, and FAANG stocks. You never cared about these things before, but if it's what your coworkers are spending a lot of time and money on, shouldn't you too?

While the largest amount of pressure comes from the sheer volume of influences in the workplace, the intensity of pressure coming from friends and family should not be overlooked. We all know the phrase "keeping up with the Joneses"—the need to own as much as our neighbors. Another popular phrase presses the point further, saying, "Too many people spend money they haven't earned to buy things they don't want to impress people they don't like."[1] Imagine how much more we'll follow the financial cues of people we actually like—our family and friends!

We discussed in the last chapter how comparing ourselves to our friends can make us discontent—and it is easy to make financial decisions based on how we want others to think of us. They also influence how we spend and invest money just like we saw in the workplace. It's important to be aware of these pressures so we can stop making decisions because we see others making them and start making decisions based on a deeper purpose.

The last source of influence on our financial decisions might surprise you. Financial institutions themselves, along with government regulation, play a surprisingly large role in how people will operate by default.

Let's begin with spending. People will spend up to the credit limit on their credit cards or make other big-ticket purchases (such as cars) based on the maximum payment they can qualify for. Others will look for a home based on the maximum amount they can borrow without even realizing it is a function of debt-to-income or mortgage-to-income—the amount lenders will offer based on their assessment of the risk you won't pay them back, not a reasonable amount based on your situation or their good desires for your finances!

You may be thinking you would never allow these things to influence how you spend money. But perhaps you make decisions based on other limits such as how much to save for retirement. Do you contribute the maximum to your 401(k) and not think about it any further? Or maybe you still contribute the default amount and haven't put in the effort to adjust it? Or maybe you donate 10 percent to charity because you think that is what you are supposed to do? (We may have finally gotten a reaction from you on that one!) Or perhaps your estate plan has been drafted solely based on the current estate tax laws and not based on serious thought about what you want to happen and why?

How did you react to these scenarios? Perhaps you're doing financial planning by default rather than making decisions. Do you spend based on a plan? Was it discussed with your spouse? If not, it is likely that there is some spending you would do differently. Or, and more importantly, have you completed estate planning documents? If not, you have made a decision: the decision to have your estate handled by state intestacy laws (laws for those who die without a will).

Why Matters

The biggest problem with managing your finances by default is that it doesn't work—except for the fortunate few who just happen to throw their dollars at the right things. We know this is the case because the world isn't full of peaceful, content, and generous people walking around financially prepared for the future. One of the most dangerous aspects of Default Financial Planning is that you won't find out you have a problem until you have just a couple ways to help alleviate the problem. For example, if you show up at our office at age sixty-five wondering if you can retire in a year or two and you've been managing your finances by default—a little savings here and there, a 401(k), maybe dabbling with trading stocks—you will likely hear some tough news. Not only would it be difficult to retire at the lifestyle you desire, but all of the options you had earlier to prepare are gone. The only option you have left is working longer since that allows you to put off spending what you have saved and potentially earn credits for delaying Social Security. Often people think they could save a large amount for only a few years, but that will have little impact over a long retirement.

To move beyond Default Financial Planning, you have to move into Purposeful Financial Planning—to put in the work of defining what you want your life to be (your ultimate purpose) and then evaluate whether your finances reflect that. It sounds like a lot, but it's not as difficult as it may seem. Aligning your finances with your values is best done over time as you reflect upon where your dollars are going. It's also best to have someone you can have candid discussions with about these topics, someone who will be able to challenge you when your actions don't align with the priorities you outlined.

Our favorite story of this comes from another financial planner whose client expressed to him that what he really wants is to spend more time with his children. Several months later that same client told him about a very expensive new car he was looking to purchase. Gently, the planner pointed out to his client that spending that much money on a car was in direct conflict with what he values since it would require more time at the office rather than with his kids. This led to an "Aha!" moment for that client which brought his spending back into alignment with what he valued most. For believers, we must also bring our spending into alignment with God's Word as we let that shape our personal desires. We will explore this deeper in Chapter 4, but for now it is sufficient to acknowledge that our faith will play a large role in determining our values and purpose and how to best use our finances in light of that.

For years, we thought that moving people from Default Financial Planning to Purposeful Financial Planning was the key to being successful planners. We even gave our business the tagline "Purposeful Wealth Management." We wanted to be clear that we wholeheartedly believed that the only way to do financial planning well was to do it with your ultimate purpose in mind at every point. We still believe this to be true, but we also realized that there was something still missing. Just knowing your purpose wasn't enough to ensure that you would be fulfilled and satisfied with your finances. We realized that we didn't want to merely help clients "build bigger barns."

3

The Safer Storeroom

The land of a rich man produced plentifully, and he thought to himself, "What shall I do, for I have nowhere to store my crops?" And he said, "I will do this: I will tear down my barns and build larger ones, and there I will store all my grain and my goods. And I will say to my soul, 'Soul, you have ample goods laid up for many years; relax, eat, drink, be merry.'" But God said to him, "Fool! This night your soul is required of you, and the things you have prepared, whose will they be." So is the one who lays up treasure for himself and is not rich toward God.[1]

THIS PARABLE OF Jesus, the parable of the rich man, is simple yet profound—and God used it to show us what a business intentionally oriented toward Him could look like.

The rich man's land was producing more than he needed, and he wondered what to do with this excess. Notice what he's missing in the beginning of this story—both an acknowledgement that this plentiful crop was a blessing from God as well as any thought about anything other than himself. The rich man thinks he has come up with a wise and prudent plan: to tear down his barns to build larger ones. We also see him reason that with so much excess stored in his barns, he will be able to relax and live the good life. Augustine, the ancient Christian philosopher,

17

commented that the farmer was "proudly disregarding all those empty bellies of the poor. He did not realize that the bellies of the poor were much safer storerooms than his barns."[2]

If you had read the first couple of verses aloud, you may have caught something that you likely missed by reading silently. Read it again and notice how many times the rich man says "I" or "my"—ten times in just a couple of sentences! Jesus is showing us that this rich man is very self-absorbed. We quickly learn what God thinks of him as he rebukes the man for his foolish thinking. He was foolish for living as if all that mattered was himself, as if God were not in control—and his finances reflected this.

Notice that he didn't sell his excess as part of his business, nor give any of it to the poor, nor give any of it to the Lord. It was all about himself, the here and now, and the good life he was storing up for himself.

After years of advising clients, we had the realization that we were helping most clients do exactly what this rich man was doing: build bigger barns, accumulate more and more, and have an illusion of control and an internal focus of obtaining the good life. In the coming chapters we share how this applies to our unique financial planning process, but before we do that, we want to share our story.

We were basically doing Default Financial Planning with our careers. We did what we thought was best for clients because it was the way we were taught to build a profitable business. We'll let you in on a little secret of running a traditional financial planning business: to maximize profit and revenue, the goal is to find as many wealthy clients as you can and, ideally, help them accumulate more and more rather than spending or giving out of their abundance. This is how you show your peers that you are a successful businessman who must be giving sage advice and perhaps they should be working with you too. It can be an addicting cycle and certainly one we didn't think we would eventually choose to step out of.

The Lord began working in our hearts to see that our job put us in a unique situation to encourage clients to live meaningful lives, not just stockpile plenty of means. We began wondering what it would look like to give advice differently. Could we help people figure out how much was enough? Could we encourage people to be more generous than they ever thought possible? We knew that if our clients lived their lives like the rich man in the parable, they would be foolish. We also concluded that if we helped our clients with this kind of life, we would be complicit in that foolishness.

> We concluded that if we helped our clients merely lay up treasures for themselves, we would be complicit in that foolishness.

Finding Our Purpose

This shift in how we gave advice did not happen overnight. We could not lead clients where we had not been ourselves. Realizing that we needed to change after we already had an established business presented some unique challenges and fear on our part. Our business had already had the tagline "Purposeful Wealth Management" for several years. It was an easy way to "put it out there" that we wanted to help people understand the purpose behind their financial decisions. Oddly enough, we did not have anyone knocking on our door searching for how to bring purpose to their finances. We also didn't see a change in our current clients or have many more purposeful conversations. We knew how much clarity it could bring from the few clients we had helped, and we struggled to think of ways we could help all of our clients find this direction.

We then found the amazingly obvious solution that took us an embarrassingly long time to realize: just ask them! We asked if some of them would be interested in gathering for dinner so we could ask them some questions related to our business. To our surprise, they all agreed, and seemed excited to help! Despite their eagerness, we were not so sure how it would go. Would they think it was weird for financial planners to talk about purpose and ask deep questions? What if they thought we were running the business all wrong?

We ended up presenting them with a one-page document with a section at the top to write a statement of purpose. This would get on paper what they were looking to accomplish with their finances. Below that are financial planning topics and action items that are influenced by the statement of purpose. The feedback we received blew us away. Not only did they like what we showed them, they encouraged us to keep leaning into this idea of purpose and how it could impact how they handled their finances. As one attender put it, "We need you to ask these questions. There isn't anyone else in my life who is going to." Another said, "Our relationship is based on trust, so we trust you to ask questions if you think they need to be asked. And don't worry about going too far. If we aren't ready to talk about it, we'll ask you to move on. But we give you permission to ask the questions."

With this validation, we were excited to bring this new page into all our clients plans and start having these conversations. The goal was to meet people where they were. Some clients were believers and would likely be very receptive to a new focus in our conversations with them, but others we knew did not claim any Christian identity. There were times the statement of purpose confused people. In these cases, a common question was: "Isn't the purpose to grow the portfolio and make sure we don't run out of money?" We will then often turn to the well-known saying "money is just a tool" to help them understand. We'll tell them that money isn't a good ultimate purpose for their lives just like collecting as many hammers as possible isn't a good ultimate purpose. Both are just tools. No one builds bigger barns just to have them full of hammers. Another way we'll use the analogy, especially when it seems to be clicking, is by talking about how tools are used to accomplish other things. When a hammer is used improperly, and it hits our fingers (far more likely to happen to Eric than Mike) and will cause harm. When amassing more is the focus of money, there is also potential for harm. Focusing on each client's purpose was a clear break from the Default Financial Planning that we discussed in the previous chapter.

As we had these conversations we began seeing patterns, especially with our clients who were believers. When Christians understand the purpose behind their finances, they begin to make decisions in a very intentional way—through a lens of stewardship, responsibility, and contentment in their hearts. Those concepts (purpose, stewardship, and contentment) are like three legs of a stool—when one of them is off, you will certainly feel pressure as you try to stay upright. This is not to say that it will come naturally. As we covered in the previous chapters, we live in a discontented culture, and we are constantly being told how we ought to use our resources. These influences give us a sort of financial amnesia that causes us to make financial decisions that are in direct conflict with what we've stated we want to do without even realizing the contradiction.

The practical chapters of this book will have stories and steps to help us handle our finances the way we actually want to. We are completely certain that this is how the Lord would have us helping others and we are excited to help you along this journey.

Let's begin. We will start by getting organized with our thoughts—similar to how we begin financial planning meetings by getting our statements and policies organized and under-standing what the client has and where it is. We don't want any ambiguity in the foundational thought process so that we can then apply it to each area of personal finances.

4

Getting Practical – Organize

EVERY TIME WE open a new account for a client there is one question we have to ask that could be a bit misleading: "What is the client's net worth?"*

It is a straightforward calculation. You simply take what you own and subtract what you owe to others. Do you know what your net worth is? Many people will keep track of this figure, either monthly or quarterly, to measure how successful they are financially—a scorecard of sorts. It is simple arithmetic, yet misleading.

We will understand net worth more clearly after the first step of financial planning: get organized. It is impossible to give good advice without having the entire picture in view. Similarly, our thoughts must be organized if we are going to truly understand what contentment and stewardship look like in all areas of our finances. Think of your financial knowledge like a jigsaw puzzle. Each thing you believe to be true is a piece in this puzzle—for example, one of your pieces might be that you think credit cards are bad. We need to make sure you have all the right pieces before we get started, because some of your pieces might have

---

* In our practice we avoid using the term "net worth" both for the reasons to follow in this chapter and because we are all worth infinitely more to our Creator than any dollar amount we could be reduced to.

come from an uncle, what you overheard on the subway, or what you've picked up by watching Shark Tank.

The Foundation

We believe the Bible is the source of truth. Not just *a* truth, but "true truth," as theologian and author Francis Schaeffer would put it.[1] This means that it is always authoritative and binding for all people. It is God revealing Himself to us through divinely inspired words. Based on biblical teaching, we believe that, ultimately, the correct answer to the net worth question is always zero. Sound crazy? Let us explain.

There are 2,350 Bible verses on money, wealth, and possessions.[2] Of those verses, dozens are about God owning it all. Genesis opens with the creation story—God creating the universe and all that is in it in six days—and as creator, he is owner. In Exodus 19:5, God tells Moses, "For all the earth is mine." Deuteronomy 10:14 says, "Behold, to the Lord your God belong heaven and the heaven of heavens, the earth with all that is in it." Psalm 24:1 tells us, "The earth is the Lord's and the fullness thereof, the world and those who dwell therein." The phrase "the earth is the Lord's and the fullness thereof" is also repeated in 1 Corinthians 10:26. From the Old Testament to the New, God's complete ownership of all creation is clear. It is a truth we must not forget because it has implications for all of life.

Owners have the right to do with their property as they please. When the owner of a sports team moves the franchise, that is their decision—certainly not the fans' decision who can't go to the games any longer nor the mayor's decision who is left with an empty stadium and lost tax revenue. It is easy for us to understand the implications of an owner's rights with this sort of example, but it can be harder to think through the implications of God owning everything.

> Since God owns it all, we have no "rights" to what we have—instead, we have responsibilities.

The first implication is that since God owns it all (and has the "rights" to it), we have no "rights" to what we have—instead, we have responsibilities. We are stewards of what He has given us. We may have the benefits of what He has given us while it is in our possession, but we do not ever have the ownership "rights." In its place we have the obligation to be good stewards of what He has entrusted us with.

R.C. Sproul, pastor and founder of Ligonier Ministries, said, "Fundamentally, stewardship is about exercising our God-given dominion over His creation."[3] This excellent definition is broad enough to cover everything God calls us to. The key to exercising that dominion properly will be through maintaining a stewardship mindset. A stewardship mindset is a complete 180-degree shift from Default Financial Planning. It looks at all financial decisions and asks if they align with God's ownership, rather than if they make me feel happy or more secure.

We will explore this in more detail in the following chapters, but we want you to know right off the bat that this is freeing and not restrictive. God hasn't made you a steward of his resources to make you live an ascetic life in which you avoid anything that has the slightest hint of enjoyment. However, there is a tension here and it will be found in chapter after chapter. Dealing with those tensions is simply part of being a steward. Consider 2 Corinthians 9:8— "And God is able to make all grace abound to you, so that having all sufficiency in all things at all times, you may abound in every good work." That is the stewardship mindset: God's blessings (all grace) supplying all our needs (all sufficiency) so that we can bless others (good works).

Simply put, we cannot be good stewards if we only have the stewardship mindset in some areas of our lives. Howard Dayton, author and founder of Compass: Finances God's Way, illustrates this idea well using an example from the Crusades (the twelfth-century religious war). The Crusaders hired mercenaries to fight for them, but before sending them into battle they would baptize each one. It was not a normal baptism, however. The mercenaries would hold their swords up to keep them from going under the water. They did not want Jesus to be Lord of their swords.

We cannot do the same with our money, holding it up out of the water to maintain control. Jesus tells us in Matthew 6:24, "No one can serve two masters, for either he will hate the one and love the other, or he will be devoted to the one and despise the other. You cannot serve God and money." While stewardship entails much more, how we handle our money is the clearest way to check ourselves if we have the correct frame of mind.

When you have a stewardship mindset, it will permeate how you speak about money and material things in such a way that it will often catch the listener off guard, even fellow believers. It is so countercultural. A pastor was once traveling to a rural part of another country and was to be picked up at the airport by a local missionary. The pastor was expecting the car to be beat up and older than he was, but he was shocked at the quality of the vehicle. As he sat down in the nice comfy passenger seat he looked at the missionary and said, "You have a nice car," to which the missionary replied, "This is God's car." If only we were all so quick to let others know who the true owner of our possessions is instead of accumulating more in hopes of gaining admiration from our peers. Perhaps then we would not hold on so tightly to our possessions and would react to loss the way John Wesley did when he learned his house had burned down: "The Lord's house burned. One less responsibility for me!"[4]

> God owns it all, which means He can do with it whatever He pleases.

Wesley's reaction leads us to the second implication of God owning everything: He can do with it whatever He pleases. Perhaps nowhere in Scripture is this clearer than Psalm 135:6—"Whatever the Lord pleases, he does, in heaven and on earth, in the seas and all deeps." Implicit to this notion is God's care and provision for any trials that might arise. God is faithful to meet our needs. This is clear throughout Scripture and should be foundational to our contentment. We can rest in this knowledge. We would do well to let these passages penetrate our souls:

Luke 12:24— "Consider the ravens: they neither sow nor reap, they have neither storehouse nor barn, and yet God feeds them. Of how much more value are you than the birds!"

Job 1:21— "And he said, 'Naked I came from my mother's womb, and naked shall I return. The Lord gave, and the Lord has taken away; blessed be the name of the Lord.'"

1 Timothy 6:8— "But if we have food and clothing, with these we will be content."

God's provision for us does not mean that we do not have a role to play. 2 Corinthians 9:8 says that God provides so we will be ready for every good work. In Luke 12:24 and 1 Timothy 6:8 we see that God is faithful to meet our needs. Basic needs like food and clothing, when not extravagant, are far different from our wants. We may want a certain job, car, or house, but by no means does God owe us those things. In fact, it just may be that having those things would keep us from being ready for "every good work."

God's provision does not mean that trials will never come our way. Isaiah 45:6-7 says, "I am the Lord, and there is no other. I form light and create darkness, I make well-being and create calamity, I am the Lord, who does all these things." In the moment of trials and difficulties it can be difficult to see God's purpose for allowing such pain in your life, but we do have the promise that it will work for good for those who love God (Romans 8:28). Nor are difficult times a free pass to be discontent. Contentment does not mean we ignore those difficult times or pretend like they are not significant issues. True contentment is resting in God's character, attributes, and promises despite those circumstances because of who God is.

We've spent most of this chapter looking at stewardship of our money. There are two more areas of stewardship we should investigate before we move to how to put this all into practice: time and talents. (Is it even biblical teaching if alliteration is not used? "Time, talents, and treasure" flows better than "time, financial resources, and personal gifts.")

Stewarding Our Time

They say time is the great equalizer. We all have twenty-four hours in a day regardless of our economic status. God gave us those twenty-four hours to accomplish what we need to do—our work, play, rest, responsibilities, sleep, and the list could go on and on. We're called to be wise in how we use our time. Ephesians 5:15-17 says, "Look carefully then how you walk, not as unwise but as wise, making the best use of the time, because the days are evil. Therefore do not be foolish, but understand what the will of the Lord is." In the following chapters of practical advice we will make reference to being good stewards of our time, especially in the chapters on career, investing, and retirement.

Stewarding Our Talents (Personal Gifts)

"So we do not focus on what is seen, but on what is unseen. For what is seen is temporary, but what is unseen is eternal" (2 Corinthians 4:18). What better way to use the talents and gifts that God has given us than for the advancement of His Kingdom? God's Kingdom, defined by author and theologian Graeme Goldsworthy, is "God's people in God's place under God's rule."[5] What is unseen is eternal and we would be wise to make investments there—not just with our treasure, but also with our time and talents—to serve the body of Christ and to reach those who do not yet know Him. This should be a staple throughout the life of a Christian, but in this book our focus will be on the role we play in our families and the local church. After this discussion on stewardship, what do you think about

29

your net worth? Will you affirm that all you have has been given to you by God, to do with as you see fit, as a steward? God may have given you little or much, but you are called to steward those possessions with contentment.

With our thoughts organized, it's time to get practical in specific areas of personal finance to see how to live out our purposes as stewards with content hearts. This will be the key to honoring God in our financial lives.

Biblically & Purposefully
The Bible is our source of truth.
God owns it all; we have responsibilities.
We can rest in God's provision, but we do have a role to play, including stewarding our resources, time, and talents.

5

Getting Practical – Work

IN 1996, A new Christian ministry to help the poor was founded in Bradford, England, with a small donation and a man following God's call on his life. His name is John Kirkby. Because of his own life story, John had a heart for those crippled by debt, who wondered where their next meal would come from and generally felt hopeless. John had overcome that life, had a good job in the finance industry, and had just gotten married when he decided to trust God's calling, leave his job, and start Christians Against Poverty (CAP).

It was an extremely difficult road starting in a one room office with practically no funding, but the work was so rewarding as John saw lives changing and people coming to faith in Christ. There was no way he could stop. Now, over twenty-five years later, CAP's Bradford office is 50,000 square feet with 300 team members, and they have expanded to Australia, New Zealand, Canada, and the United States. John was even honored by the late Queen Elizabeth II as Commander of the Most Excellent Order of the British Empire presented in person by the then Prince Charles![1]

No doubt this is a remarkable story about what God can do through a man's work life, but are all Christians to go on the same journey that John took? Are all Christians called to find work that advances the Kingdom?

31

We think this is a key question that all believers should consider and answer. This chapter is strategically placed here— right after organizing our thoughts around what God says about money and before we get to topics like debt, lifestyle, generosity, or retirement. This is because we know that a wrong view of work will inevitably flow into wrong views about what to do with the fruit of your work (cash flow), how long to work

> A misunderstanding of work spreads into misunderstanding in many other areas.

(retirement), and what to do with the fruit of your work when you are gone (legacy). It is like a cancer, spreading into other areas of your life.

So, as you read this chapter, we encourage you to consider these words in light of where you are in your career. Perhaps there is far less road ahead of you than behind you. If so, consider how you will end strong as well as your timeline and motivation. For those already retired, reflect on this view of work compared to how you viewed it when you started your career. What did you get right and wrong? Who could you share that with to encourage them to view their vocation biblically? What work are you doing now?

What Does the Bible Teach about Work?

Randy Alcorn, in his fantastic book *Money, Possessions, and Eternity*, wrote, "Work is the God-ordained means for contributing to society, finding fulfillment, and meeting material needs so we can provide for our families." This is a great definition because, not only is it biblical, but it is all-encompassing—young or old, highly skilled or not, even doing very simple or unpaid work—all workers are included. Let's dive into that definition and see the biblical principles at work, expand upon those principles, and then see the applications.

What Do We Mean by "God-Ordained"?

We should clarify some assumptions behind the phrase "God-ordained" to help us understand the rest of that definition. Genesis 1:1 tells us that God created the heavens and the earth. God did not have to create anything, but He did so for the joy of it, because he is a creator God. Not only is all that He created called "good," but the act of creating, or working, is itself good. We can also see that in Genesis 2:15, which says, "The Lord God took the man and put him in the garden of Eden to work it and keep it." This is before the fall (Genesis 3), so we see that work itself is good.

We're also told that God made man "in his own image." Our creator God, who finds joy in His work, made it part of His perfect design that we would work and create as well. It is part of who we are because it is a part of who God is. Jesus said to the Jewish religious leaders who were upset that he was healing on the Sabbath, "My Father is working until now, and I am working" (John 5:17). God's work did not stop after creation. It is a part of who He is, for His joy and glory, and so His work continues. Perhaps our work should not stop either (more on that in Chapter 8). For now, it is enough to see that work is both normative and pleasing to God.

Work as a God-Ordained Means for "Contributing to Society"

The key to this part of our definition is that work is not about us. Sometimes simple truths are easy to overlook, but we should not skip past this too quickly. With what we've said so far about work, you should have no difficulty seeing how God views our work as meant for others. This narrowly includes family, which is later in our definition, but it also more broadly includes society. Because of the fall, several things happened to work. Not only did work become difficult (along with all the problems that come from that), but it also became a way we could be selfish. As sinners in a fallen world, we will not be able to remove all the selfish ways we use work. But we must regain the perspective that work is not ultimately for us, lest it become an idol that keeps us from fully worshiping God.

"Contributing to society" refers to all that is needed for a society to function. The definition we're using does not say work is the God-ordained means for "contributing to the church" or "feeding the hungry" or "caring for the poor"—all necessary and good things that are included in society, but not the only concern. In 1967, Dr. Martin Luther King, Jr. gave a speech at a junior high school and said, "If it falls to your lot to be a street sweeper, sweep streets like Michelangelo painted pictures, sweep streets like Beethoven composed music, sweep streets like Leontyne Price sings before the Metropolitan Opera. Sweep streets like Shakespeare wrote poetry. Sweep streets so well that all the hosts of heaven and earth will have to pause and say: Here lived a great street sweeper who swept his job well."[2] Dr. King's view aligns more closely with the Bible than the false idea that all believers ought to be in full-time ministry.

There are many Scripture passages on work, but two stand out as particularly applicable here. Colossians 3:23-24 tells us to work with all our hearts for we are serving the Lord, and 1 Thessalonians 4:11-12 tells us to work humbly so that others may see our example. We have had clients who were believers handle this tension very well. They understood their gifts and abilities gave them careers with incomes that allowed them to be very generous, working behind the scenes supporting their church and other ministries. They also were effective witnesses in the workplace. As Christians, we ought to work in ways that honor God. We must keep the focus on God and off of ourselves.

Work as a God-Ordained Means for "Finding Fulfillment"

Work is the God-ordained means for finding fulfillment. What does that mean? It doesn't mean that work is our only source of fulfillment—we know that is not true. But God did make us to find fulfillment in a job well done. Perhaps this is why both of us enjoy mowing our lawns. There is joy and fulfillment in seeing a job well done. Proverbs 13:4 tells us, "The soul of the sluggard craves and gets nothing, while the soul of the diligent is richly supplied."

The sluggard does not complete his work and has no fulfillment, while the diligent completes his work and is satisfied. Reflect on your life and others you know and you will see how God uses work to give us fulfillment. Another way to think about this is that we find fulfillment in work because God uses work to build our character. Peter tells us that God uses suffering for our good and our godliness (1 Peter 4); similarly, our character will be refined as we seek to honor God in how we work.

Work as a God-Ordained Means for "Meeting Material Needs So We Can Provide for Our Families"

As we saw earlier, we have very clear biblical teaching on the importance of work to meet our needs and caring for our families. We can see in Proverbs 20 that work is connected to material needs: "The sluggard does not plow in the autumn; he will seek at harvest and have nothing." Perhaps Paul had this in mind when he told the Thessalonians that "if anyone is not willing to work, let him not eat" (note that *willingness* to work is the determining factor, not *ability*). Work is how God intends our material needs to be met.

Paul also wrote to Timothy, "But if anyone does not provide for his relatives, and especially for members of his household, he has denied the faith and is worse than an unbeliever." It does not get much clearer than this: believers are to work to provide all necessities for their families. This has nothing to do with lifestyle (we'll get to that later), so you can't use it as a reason to convince your spouse you need to take that Caribbean vacation.

The Default View of Work

The paragraphs above are starkly different from our culture's general view of work, with the exception of working hard.

Everything else has been turned upside down because God's plan for work has been replaced with selfish desires. In this world, there is pride in the number of hours worked, the number of nights spent in hotels on business trips, or becoming a "million miler" on your preferred airline. Stephen Hawking said, "Work gives you meaning and purpose and life is empty without it."[3] With this view of work, contributing to society is traded in for contributing to one's own desires. Wealth is the most common goal, but status, promotions, and prestige are just as powerful motivations for some.

> With this view of work, contributing to society is traded in for contributing to one's own desires.

This view is perfectly shown in *Fortune's Children: The Fall of the House of Vanderbilt*, in which Arthur T. Vanderbilt II writes of his ancestor Cornelius "the Commodore" Vanderbilt, "It was not what he could do with his money that interested the Commodore. It was the money itself. The money. It was money madness, greed. The money was the basis of his self-esteem, it was his tally of his wins, of his success, of his self-worth, and there would never be enough to satisfy him." The Commodore's view represents the default view of work because he sees no distinction between his job and its outcomes—money, self-worth, and prestige. The work or how it was performed didn't matter, just the outcomes. How much did you make? How do you compare to others? How do they view you? The only time other people come into the equation is as a comparison to yourself.

However, it is common to see the biblical model of work as a source of fulfillment twisted into work becoming an idol.

John Calvin famously said, "The human heart is an idol factory."[4] God created us to worship Him, but when we deny Him we end up worshiping something else. For most, that means worshiping money. For some it is family, and for others it is work. They look to work for satisfaction, which will inevitably lead to significant disappointment when things go wrong. Trials of life always come—perhaps an economic downturn or being laid off—and then where will they turn?

Finally, we see that work as a God-ordained means for meeting material needs can transform into a way to meet every material *want*. This is different from the influences we discussed in the Default Financial Planning chapter where we desire what others have. It is also different from lifestyle creep—spending more money as your income increases—that will be discussed later on. This is working simply to get more for yourself—more wealth, more toys. This can sometimes happen through overworking, when you put in more hours to earn more money at the loss of other things in your life. More commonly, it can be through climbing the corporate ladder, always looking for what comes next and the compensation that comes with it. The new job could bring more stress, longer hours, and more travel away from home, but if the money increases many think it's worth it. Often this desire for more, which comes with a cost in other areas of life, is "sanitized" by calling it ambition. Ambition is a good thing, so making these trade-offs must be good too, right?

Proper Ambition

There is a right way and a wrong way to use ambition, just like there is a right and wrong way to eat an Oreo (Google it—according to the Oreo team there is a right way). If we think of ambition as simply a desire to improve, what's the harm in that? But we must ask *what* we want to improve and *why*. In the paragraph above, we saw ambition as the desire to improve one's finances, prestige at work, or status in the community. This is the opposite of what we're told in Philippians 2:3— "Do nothing out of selfish ambition or conceit, but in humility count others more significant than yourselves." In this section of Scripture, Paul is encouraging unity, humility, and service, the opposite of selfish ambition. The biblical teaching on ambition is to live quiet lives (1 Thess. 4:11) that are pleasing to the Lord (2 Cor. 5:9). We ought to be looking for ways to serve others, just as Christ came not to be served, but to serve (Matt. 20:28).

If your ambition is to grow in your career so that you can contribute more and provide more, you are on the right path. If your ambition is to advance your career to influence others for Christ and to have more resources to help further His Kingdom, you are doing well. If, on the other hand, your ambition is to advance your career for selfish reasons, then you ought to reconsider. Perhaps the story of Pratyush Buddiga will be helpful.

From a young age, Pratyush was driven to succeed. He was also committed to rationality and dismissed religion. He said that those who went to church on Sundays "wasted their time while I zoomed ahead, victories and accolades piling up in the real world ." Intelligent and driven, Pratyush began playing poker, and by 2015 was ranked number two in the world. "One of the rational things I wanted to do was make as much money as possible and retire at a young age," he said, but this effort cost him a relationship and soon much more.

When he was nearing his financial goals (before the age of thirty), a series of losses compounded by more aggressive play led Pratyush into a bad place. Heavy eating, drinking, partying, and gambling used up 90 percent of his wealth over just a few months. He was depressed, overweight, and nearly broke. "The pursuit of money, and money alone, has many fellow travelers," he says, and one of those fellow travelers (and professional poker players) had been where Pratyush was and helped him get back on track.

He began playing well again but decided to retire from poker before reaching his financial goals. He soon found himself in the cryptocurrency and venture capital world, back on track to meet his goal of retiring young. By late 2017, Bitcoin was rocketing toward $20,000, taking Pratyush's personal wealth with it. "Poker had desensitized me enough to money that even the daily 20-30% swings in net worth that I was taking in the height of the mania in late 2017-2018 felt like nothing. I just had to bet more to win more. If I played the next 6 months right, I could make life-changing amounts of money and be done working for life. I hit my peak net worth sometime in January 2018 and glory seemed right around the corner." Then the market crashed and Pratyush's personal life went right back to where he had been several years earlier. "I kept trading, but watched my net worth slowly get decimated over the course of 2018. I initially kept up many of the practices I'd learned from podcasts: the weird stew of Buddhism, Stoicism, and rationality that attracts many high-performing males who realize that wealth and success has not granted them the happiness they thought they'd find. However, as things continued to worsen for me in life, I couldn't help but notice that these practices offered me little solace."

Pratyush then met Gwen, who is now his wife. Gwen invited Pratyush to go to church with her and over the next several months, the rationalist who thought religion was for weak-minded people accepted Jesus as his Savior. Pratyush began to think about what was next for his life. He wanted to be sure that Christ was at the center of whatever he did. Initially he thought that the only way to do that was to work in ministry. However, Pratyush came to realize "that all of us can serve Him and help bring the Kingdom of Heaven to Earth, either inside or outside the church. As I prayed about it, I became increasingly certain that the world of technology was the one I was called to be in."

This is not to diminish the idea of going into full-time ministry at all. We've had clients leave the corporate world to go into full-time ministry and it is a joy for us to play a small role in helping make that happen. For those of us who have not felt God calling us in that direction, we want to offer Pratyush's example of how to bring your faith into whatever you do for work. Pratyush's view of work changed completely: "Instead of hunting for status and wealth or identity in what I'm investing in, I am secure in my identity in Christ. He knows me, sees me, and loves me. That makes me free to work with the people I want to work with, invest in the people and technology I believe in, and avoid the pitfalls that have tripped me up before. I want firstly to serve others, shunning glory and holding the admiration and status games of the world at bay. Those can come and go, but what remains is stewardship and our dutifulness to what God has put in our hands."[5]

Pratyush summarizes a biblical view of work well, but there are other things we can add. He mentions stewardship and that can be expanded upon. When it comes to work, we can steward the finances and resources of our employer, our time, and our talents.

Christian employees should steward their company's resources well. Among the benefits of this is the witness it is to your coworkers. Maybe they will also notice other things you steward well. It is a powerful witness to have convictions about how you spend your time and then to live it out, even when there is a cost. Think about the flip side of this as well: if you have a family at home and your coworkers know they see you more than your children do, what message does that send?

> Remember that God does not view our 9-5 any differently than any other part of our lives.

Stewarding talents means that you are utilizing the gifts that God has given you. It would be wise to use your unique talents at work—if you are strong with numbers but pursue the arts, it might not be a wrong decision, but it just may not be the wisest choice. As members of the body of Christ, we have all been given gifts to serve the body. To do this, you need to steward your time well in order to have time to be useful to the local church.

Finally, contentment is hinted at above, but we should be clear: in the workplace, we have a great opportunity to show where we put our faith by how we react to the difficulties that will arise. Our security in Christ and the knowledge of His care for us allows us to be content and keep our heads when everything around us is in a frenzy.

Do these qualities sound like your view of work? Remember that God does not view our 9-5 any differently than any other part of our lives. It is to be subject to Christ and for His glory. We should be productive, generous, and content stewards providing for our families and looking for ways to share and demonstrate the love of Christ. If you take on the world's view of work, you will inevitably view the fruit of your work, your cash flow, the same way. That is what we will look at next.

Default Financial Planning	Biblically & Purposefully
Leisure is normative; work is for more leisure	Work is normative
Contribute to my desires – wealth, status	Contribute to society and the local church
Ultimate satisfaction found in work	Find fulfillment – a job well done, character built
Meet material wants	Meet material needs

6

Getting Practical – Cash Flow

WE'VE ALL HEARD the stories about professional athletes who earn millions of dollars yet find themselves bankrupt just a few years after retiring. There's much that can be said about these cases, but it is safe to say that a core issue was a complete misunderstanding of cash flow. We shouldn't just pick on athletes, however—celebrities have had their share of financial missteps. One famous recording artist found herself in financial trouble and decided to sue her financial advisor. His response: "Was it really necessary to tell her that if you spend money on things, you will end up with the things and not the money?" The rest of us might not have the same number of actual dollars to spend, but the necessity of making wise decisions is universal.

Cash flow refers to what you do with your money—your lifestyle. We use the terms interchangeably, but both refer to the four basic ways money can be used. Money is a tool with four basic uses. Ron Blue uses a memorable motto to describe these in *Master Your Money*: LIVE, GIVE, OWE, GROW.

LIVE – This is money you spend on your living expenses, which is a broad category that ranges from the gas you put in your car to clothes for your family to entertainment. It also includes the principal paid on your mortgage or other debts.

GIVE – This covers anything you give away—mostly gifts to your church and other charities but also includes gifts to other people or family members.

OWE – This is money owed to someone else. Taxes are usually the most significant part of this category, but it also includes interest payments (mortgage, auto, or other types of loans).

GROW – This includes anything you are saving—funds accumulated at your bank, saved for college, or put in your retirement accounts.

In this chapter, we are going to spend time on each of those four categories—giving as much insight and practical advice as we can—but we will not be giving recommended percentages to allocate resources to them. We believe that is far too personal and can vary widely based on your current situation. This is where, as we mentioned in Chapter 2, you will do well to reflect over time on where your dollars are going and have the input of someone you trust. Toward the end of the chapter, we will give you a quick and easy way to calculate what percentage of your income falls into each category. Often seeing these percentages will be eye-opening and helpful as you begin to be more intentional in where you allocate your cash flow.

This chapter will likely require the hardest work for you to do as you begin to align your beliefs and purpose with the way you use money each day. This is to be expected since the four uses of money are all competing for the same dollars. You will feel the tension. There is also not much gray area when looking at cash flow—the numbers are what they are. Cash flow is a key consideration when judging the health of businesses or investments.

Personal cash flow is also a key consideration when judging how well you are stewarding what God has given you. We aren't going for a AAA rating from a credit agency, we are seeking "well done good and faithful servant" from our Creator (Matt. 25:23). But don't let that overwhelm you.

Remember that our God is loving, patient, and kind and has a lot more grace than an analyst from Moody's or Standard & Poor's!

One more thing to keep in mind is that contentment is going to be front and center in many cash flow decisions. Consider this illustration: if you are discontent with the money you have in your LIVE category, you will likely take on more debt. That can be as "tame" as a car loan or an above average mortgage balance or as extreme as credit card debt. This debt keeps you from saving and investing (the GROW category) which often leads to either a lack of giving or giving out of obligation (without joy). This is not a cycle that you want to find yourself in and contentment will be your greatest weapon to fight that trap.

> Remember that our God is loving, patient, and kind and has a lot more grace than an analyst from Moody's or Standard & Poor's!

So many of us long for contentment but find it elusive. We could chalk it up to the curse of sin and living in a fallen world, but as you read the rest of this chapter, consider the roles that fear and the love of money play into your decisions. Hebrews 13:5–6 explains this connection: "Keep your life free from love of money and be content with what you have, for he has said, 'I will never leave you nor forsake you.' So we can confidently say, 'The Lord is my helper; I will not fear; what can man do to me?'"

In this passage, we see a connection made between not loving money and contentment with what we have. This is easy to follow—if we don't love money or things, we can be content with our situation. But then the passage shifts to remind us that God will never forsake us and that we should not fear. Many, however, trust in money and not God. They feel safe and secure because of the balances in their accounts, suppressing the knowledge that money fails quickly and ultimately since it cannot buy them more time here on earth. When money fails them, fear is left. But God enables us not to fear and below we hope to help you make that a reality in your life.

Finally, if you are retired, this is still relevant to you so keep reading! Sure, you may not be saving any longer and you may not have any debts, but you still have a decision to make between how much cash flow to allocate for living versus giving away.

LIVE

How much of your income should go toward your living expenses? This is not a simple question. Ask ten of your friends and you'll likely get ten different answers! As we mentioned, we will not be giving percentage recommendations or even rules of thumb about this. Perhaps there would be some benefit to knowing that Americans spend an average of 4.93 percent of their income on utilities, but we believe it is far more valuable to think through some principles and develop convictions about how much you want to spend on any given budget item.

Let's start with how someone doing Default Financial Planning would determine how much to live on. Our culture confuses having money with spending money. It is so ingrained in us that whenever we see someone with nice things, we assume they are rich. Morgan Housel has pointed out that most people say that they want to be millionaires, but they actually mean they want to spend millions of dollars

> Our culture confuses having money with spending money.

and don't realize that those things are literally opposites. By default, most people determine their spending by their income. It's automatic with no thought or plan. This is dangerous because it is easy to fake it when their income doesn't match the lifestyle they want. Others who have similar finances see the mirage and think they can spend that way, too. Or perhaps it is covetousness that drives this cycle of spending what they earn.

Hopefully, having read the foundation chapter, you're able to see some of the problems with handling your finances this way. To start, it is completely focused on self, and we know that we are rather to steward the money that God has entrusted to us. Default spending has no plan either. Contrast that with what Scripture tells us, that "the plans of the diligent lead surely to abundance, but everyone who is hasty comes only to poverty" (Proverbs 21:5). We once received a call just days before the tax filing deadline from someone looking for ways to lower their income to reduce their tax bill. This man had not made a plan and was therefore going to be stuck with a large tax bill.

Another attribute of spending money like this is the prominence of pride. Pride is perhaps the driving force behind the idea that to have money is to spend money. It is a desire to be seen, hoping that others will respect and admire you and make all kinds of other flattering assumptions about you.

C.S. Lewis said, "Pride gets no pleasure out of having something, only out of having more of it than the next man."[1] God calls us not to be proud, but rather humble. "God opposes the proud but gives grace to the humble" (James 4:6).

> The goal is to be consistently biblical and faithful in our choices.

Stewards. Contented. Humble. This is what we're called to, but how can our lifestyles reflect this? We believe this is best achieved through being in the Word, prayer, and partnership with someone you trust. Several of the verses we mentioned come from Proverbs, and there are many more we could have used that have the same sage advice. Proverbs is not an instruction manual; it gives principles to apply to life that may vary quite a bit from person to person. The goal is to be consistently biblical and faithful in our choices.

To help you on this journey, here are a few of the most common ways we advise on this topic:

1. Start early and control "lifestyle creep." Lifestyle creep happens when you continually increase your standard of living each year or with each pay increase without even noticing. You no longer make a choice about how you will live—it just becomes second nature to spend more. The lack of purpose behind the decision can become a significant problem. When trials happen, an expensive lifestyle can make the situation worse, especially since it is extremely hard for people to take a

step back in their standard of living. By being intentional with one's lifestyle and having a plan in place, managing these sorts of situations becomes easier. For example, college graduates have spent the last four years with a relatively low standard of living and keeping that same lifestyle even after getting their first job will set them up for good habits (a good balance of the four uses of money) that will last a lifetime.

For those fortunate enough to avoid any hiccups along the way, the problem with lifestyle creep often shows up later in life in the form of insufficient savings for their desired lifestyle in retirement. We have seen families come to us after years of consistently contributing 10 percent of their income to their retirement accounts only to find that they are under-funded. Yes, they may have amassed a decently sized portfolio, but their lifestyle costs are very high since their income is the highest it's ever been and they are spending a significant portion of it. The retirement portfolio will not be able to keep up with their ever-rising living expenses.

> A wise steward plans for the future while being content and generous in the present.

Having a plan can help prevent problems. It is important to put some thought into what you are doing now and what the impact of that will be in 5, 10, or 15 years. A wise steward plans for the future while being content and generous in the present.

Is it too late for you to start early? Not at all! Start doing what you can now and share your mistakes with your children or grandchildren.

2. It is often said, "It is easier to get rich than stay rich." Those with the responsibility of wealth also need to be mindful of lifestyle risks. We have seen the truth of this quote several times. The difficulty for some is that the actions that lead to wealth (taking risks, concentrated assets—a business or company stock for example, etc.) are usually not prudent long term. One client found this out not from taking risks, but from not controlling lifestyle. She was an executive for a Fortune 500 company who had decided to spend the tail end of her career on a startup. She had never had an advisor and began working with us at this time. She had more money than ever before and her lifestyle made it incredibly hard to scale back spending until the startup was established.

The income was going to come eventually, and she believed there was so much potential that what they were spending was nothing compared to what would come in just a few years. Their current expenses only climbed higher: a home for a child, high-end auto leases, and other unforeseen expenses hit them hard. Several years passed with some success in the startup, but the high living expenses had drained half of their investment accounts.

The pitfalls are different for those with wealth or who are already retired, but the necessity of being purposeful and having a plan remain.

3. Your success with the LIVE category will have far less to do with external factors, such as your income or where you live, than with the internal contentment you have in your heart. Remember that you are stewarding your income. You may look strange to friends or colleagues because you are not spending

like they are—and that's okay. You can be confident in the plan you have in place. You can be winsome for Christ because you do not fear money failing you and because you are humble in a world where pride usually drives lifestyle choices.

But make sure it is true humility, not the "humility" of a multi-millionaire driving a Honda Civic with 200,000 miles who tells everyone about what great financial decisions he's making. Don't be that guy.

GIVE

The Bible has much to say about giving and generosity. You might think that would mean there is a consensus on the topic, but what would be the fun in that? Throughout history some have taken advantage of others by using Scripture incorrectly, some have been well-meaning but taught unbiblical ideas, some have been legalistic while others erred by failing to teach about giving, and finally some have quibbled over the smallest differences of opinion. We have our convictions, but we will keep our consideration on principles instead of specifics to keep the focus on what matters most. At the end of the book, we have a list of resources for more specific reading on these topics.

Those operating out of Default Financial Planning tend to view giving as something that is done with "leftover" dollars. If there is anything left after LIVE, GROW, and OWE, then they give some. This giving usually doesn't have much purpose behind it. A year-end mailing or perhaps a family friend going on a mission trip may generate a gift, but it is more reactionary than intentional. This sort of giving tends to be obligatory rather than from a generous mindset that seeks out opportunities. This kind of giving also tends to be done without joy and, as we will soon see, joy will be a key indicator for us as we consider our giving.

Reflect on the giving pattern when operating by default. Giving to fund ministries and share the love of Christ should be personally exciting and inspiring for those not in full-time ministry. But often the tension of managing cash flow, along with a misunderstanding of what the Bible teaches about giving, can prevent us from being joyful givers.

> We are to be generous because God has been generous to us.

The first thing we must keep in mind is that we are to be generous because God has been generous to us. We aren't supposed to give only when we've satisfied most of our other desires and we have some funds leftover. Giving generously doesn't happen if we just give 10 percent of our income and then go back to what we really want to spend our money on. God gave his Son for us. It is his good pleasure to give us the Kingdom. Therefore, we are to be marked by generosity—living with open hands, not holding tightly to what we think is ours.

God loves a cheerful giver. As you reflect on your cash flow, and perhaps as you discuss your giving with a close friend, consider how much joy you have in your giving. 2 Corinthians 9:6–7 tells us, "The point is this: whoever sows sparingly will also reap sparingly, and whoever sows bountifully will also reap bountifully. Each one must give as he has decided in his heart, not reluctantly or under compulsion, for God loves a cheerful giver." Do you feel like you are cheerful in your giving?

Pastor Jim Johnston has written about how joy is like a gauge on the dashboard of the Christian life and uses the example of the canary. Canaries were taken into coal mines because they are very sensitive to air quality. As long as the canaries kept singing and chirping, the miners knew the air was safe from carbon monoxide and methane that they could not detect themselves. Pastor Johnston writes, "Christian joy is like that singing, yellow bird. When that bird stops singing, that is a warning to watch your life and doctrine closely."[2] It is hard for Satan to tempt a joyful giver with the empty pleasures of this world.

This is easy to understand in theory, but how do we put it into practice? What practical steps can you take to improve your use of the GIVE category? Plan! Yes, we know that, as financial planners, the answer "make a plan" is like answering "Jesus" in Sunday School. But consider our clients, Ron and Barbara. They had significant wealth and lived modestly compared to the size of their portfolio. During one of our review meetings we showed them projections of what their assets would grow to over the next twenty years based on how much they were currently spending. The significant assets were projected to become substantially more significant. Everyone knew that it was too much to leave to their children. It seemed inevitable that there would need to be a revision to their estate plan to handle large bequests to charity when they passed—that is, until we showed them what it would look like to make large gifts now, well above their "normal" giving. They had not realized they were in a position to make gifts of that size immediately and seeing it in their plan gave them the confidence to move forward. They began seeking opportunities for what the Lord would have them do with these funds and it brought joy into the process.

Earlier in this chapter we talked about how you cannot be content if you have a love of money. There is no better way to break the power of money over you than to be generous. Give it away. A generous person is free from the love of money. We also mentioned how the love of money comes from fear. We naturally want to be safe and secure and instead of trusting in the Lord—our helper who promises to care for us—we trust in money. You can't ultimately be trusting in money if you are actively giving it away.

Consider Janice Worth. Orphaned at a young age, Janice believed it was up to her to make it in this world, to make enough money to have the stability that her childhood didn't have. Driven to make this happen, she graduated from high school at sixteen, went straight to college, and then to New York City to conquer the business world. By twenty-five she owned a beauty company and several years after that she and a partner had the first infomercial ever to bring in $100 million. She was young and wealthy and her dreams had all come true, but she was still searching for something more. Eventually, she found Jesus and her life was changed. Soon after that she found herself on the new stewardship committee at her church and learned that God owned it all. Janice said, "I realized that money and possessions are what made me feel worthy and valuable. God was showing me that my zeroes were my god and what I looked to as my true savior."[3] She began the journey of living a generous life and has not looked back—not only in her personal giving but also by inspiring others to join her on that journey.

When you hear Janice tell her story, her joy in giving is front and center. When thinking about our roles as stewards, it can be easy to think in terms of "have to" rather than "get to." It is why, up until now, we have avoided using the word "tithe." It feels like such a "have to" word. Our hope is that you see that you *get* to be generous. What you *have* to do is pay what you owe to others.

OWE

The OWE category might sound far less interesting than the other categories, but there are some important issues to look at.

Taxes will be in everyone's OWE category. Income, real estate, and investment taxes are included here (sales tax we include in the LIVE category since it is directly tied to what you purchase). The level of control you have over these taxes will vary and there is certainly nothing wrong with taking advantage of strategies to lower your tax obligation.

> The amount of taxes we owe is reflective of the blessings God has given us.

But the Bible is very clear that we are to pay what we owe. Romans 13:7 says, "Pay to all what is owed to them: taxes to whom taxes are owed." There are many other Scriptures we could turn to, but don't miss that paying taxes is nothing new. By and large, the amount of taxes we owe is reflective of the blessings God has given us. It is not something to endlessly complain about to anyone who will listen. Even if you don't like how the tax dollars are being used, you still owe them and it is because of God's blessing upon you. Do you think the early Christians liked how the Roman government was using their tax dollars? They still were called to pay tax to whom tax is owed. The only surefire way to reduce these taxes is to have less income (less income tax), own a less valuable home or live in a less desirable area (lower real estate tax), or have fewer investments (and therefore less tax, although in the next chapter we will see that this is where you have more control). These are all blessings, so let us not be a grumbling people.

A more significant concern is debt, since the interest we pay on our debts are included in the OWE category. The default view of debt is that it is completely normal and the only way to live in the modern world. It has become normalized as the only way to graduate from school and the only way to buy a car or home. Most people would acknowledge that credit card debt isn't great, but many still carry a balance. What do you think about debt?

The Bible does not speak directly to debt very often. We are given a warning that the borrower is the slave of the lender (Proverbs 22:7). This does not mean debt is wrong, but this is a strong warning. We don't think that debt can be a sin since there are passages giving instructions for lending, and lending requires that someone is going into debt. We believe that the best way to consider the debt issue is through the lens of contentment and stewardship.

We once worked with a family that had put everything they had into starting a business. They knew the space well and saw a real opportunity that they couldn't pass up. You've probably heard stories like this and might be expecting to hear that their business failed. That is not this story. It went well for them—really well. The business grew so quickly that they soon needed a large office space and lots of equipment for all the new employees they were hiring. Just as they started the business with debt, they expanded with debt, too. All the profits went into expanding the business. They also lived the lifestyle you'd expect of successful business owners. This, however, was also largely funded with debt. While we worked with them, we got stressed just thinking about the risk of it all blowing up—due to one bad quarter, supply issues, inflation, wage pressures, whatever it might be. We have no idea how they lived with that much financial stress in their lives. Putting the issue of using debt for business aside, there is much to be learned from this family around the use of debt. Also set aside the home buying and mortgage debt issue for now. We will come back to that later on.

The use of debt was so normalized that it funded their lifestyle. Simply put, this means they were borrowing money to buy things they wanted because they did not have the cash today. This type of borrowing implies that we need more than God has provided for us. This is discontentment. It is poor stewardship as well—if you are funding a lifestyle with debt there is hardly any chance that your other uses of money are healthy.

Debt funding lifestyle is also dangerous. It will cause worry and stress, harming your mental health. It allows you to deny the reality of your situation in the short term but sets you up for much more severe issues in the future. What would happen if you don't have the income in the future to pay the debt back? Often people take out loans with the thought that their upcoming raise or bonus can be used to pay it off. Be wary of making such presumptions about the future.

Using debt to fund lifestyle reflects an internal issue of discontentment. More income is not likely to solve the problem.

When wants, not needs, are driving debt, more income will likely lead to bigger wants and therefore bigger debts because people feel like they must keep up appearances.

Clearly, we are not on board with debt to fund lifestyle, but what about other types of debt? Unfortunately, there are no hard and fast rules that we can offer. There are some principles that would be prudent to consider before taking on debt. You must weigh the outcomes. For example, consider student loans—some are certainly worth it while others are not. It depends on the cost of the degree and the expected income afterwards. There may be more non-financial considerations that are involved, so prayer and discernment will be essential. Also consider the impact the loan payment will have on your cash flow and each category you use money on. You do not want to have your OWE category putting pressure on other categories. Contentment is the key to this balance, remembering that nothing is eternal and no "thing" can bring us true joy.

Whenever discussing the OWE category, mortgages are the most common question. Everyone agrees on the necessity of housing and in most cases that will require a mortgage. This does not negate the need to ask some of the questions about the size of the mortgage payment and if it is a prudent amount to borrow. Too large of a mortgage payment is an extremely common problem with a very difficult solution.

Others will want advice about when they should pay off their mortgage. Our typical advice is to pay off the loan as soon as practical. For some with large portfolios, this will depend on the taxes owed, so perhaps it is done over several years. For others, it may mean adding several hundred dollars per month of principal payments. It always depends on the personal situation since there can be unintended consequences if things are done without consideration. The four categories need to be in harmony, even with worthwhile goals like reducing debt. We have seen many clients choose to pay off debt at an accelerated pace and only once has it caused any issues. We had a client who was driven to have no mortgage as soon as possible. He was only in his forties, so his only option at the time was to increase his monthly payments. He took his cash flow to essentially two categories, LIVE and OWE. He was aggressive and had the loan paid off in his fifties. The problem, other than not being generous with what the Lord had blessed him with, was that he now had college-aged children but no college savings. He also found himself well behind where he needed to be for achieving his retirement goals. A lot of equity in his house, but not much else, left him in a difficult position. There are always tradeoffs, but to be good stewards we must look at the whole picture and not become hyper-focused on a singular issue.

We want to end this category with encouragement. We have never had a client pay off a loan and regret the decision later. Even in cases where the interest rate was low and an argument could be made for keeping the debt, we have not seen regret in paying it off. It is freeing to have no debt and often there are meaningful impacts beyond the balance sheet.

GROW

There are generally two default ways people tend to think about saving and growing their money for the future. One group puts it off. They are living for the here and now and don't want to rob themselves of joys today when no one knows what tomorrow will bring. This is the "eat, drink, and be merry for tomorrow we may die" crowd. The other group wants to save as much as they can because they think that the larger their investment balance is, the happier they will be. This group identifies with Warren Buffett when he said, "Money is not everything. Make sure you earn a lot before speaking such nonsense."

How are good stewards supposed to think about saving for the future? In our human condition, we see the appeal in each of the default options people take. Our goal in this chapter has been to show you how we are called to balance the four categories, and in this section we want to encourage you along the narrow path of saving. Fall off to the left and you're in danger of being in need; fall off to the right and you're in danger of trusting in money instead of God.

We want to be very clear that we do not believe the Bible teaches that, out of the fear of loving money, you should not save or invest for the future. There are many verses we could use to show or imply that saving and investing is a good thing. Consider that Jesus spoke illustratively of investing in the parable of the talents (Matt. 25). It seems highly unlikely that Jesus would speak in a positive view of investing if it were something wicked. The issue with the love of money is when we trust in the money and not God. Fear makes us do this foolish thing. But we are not called to fear—God is our helper. He is for us and with us. Guard against trusting in money and you will be free to save and invest with purpose.

Invest with Purpose

You need to know what you are saving for. If you cannot think of something, then that dollar shouldn't be going to the GROW category. The first step is saving for an emergency fund. We all need a certain amount of funds set aside (perhaps in a high yield savings account) to be able to weather life's storms that can't be met with our normal monthly income or in the event of job loss. This number will vary depending on your circumstances, but three-to-six months' worth of expenses is the usual advice.

Once you have that in place, you can begin allocating your GROW dollars toward other goals. Traditionally, these are things like college and retirement, but it can be anything you desire or need to save for. Retirement is complex enough that it will be covered in depth in Chapter 8. College savings is also complex, but at least you usually know how long it will last. The advice is the same regardless of the goal (saving for college, a new home, medical expenses for aging parents, etc.). You must come up with the size of the expense. For college, perhaps you decide to save fifty percent of expected cost, then after making a few assumptions you know how much you need to save. This allows you to track your progress and makes it more likely that you will meet your goal.

Knowing the purpose behind your saving also allows you to be a better steward. Once a goal is met or on pace to be met, future savings can start to go elsewhere. You can also invest more prudently when you align the type of investment with the size and duration of the expense (more on this in the next chapter).

One caveat is that you don't know what changes will happen in your life or how your thinking will change in the future. A health change to you or someone in your family can drastically change your financial needs. Or perhaps in your thirties you thought you would want to work until you were at least 70, since that is common in your industry and you enjoy what you do. As a result, you save minimally for retirement, but then in your fifties you feel called to use your skills in ministry. Without savings to provide that flexibility, you may feel stuck in your job.

We have had multiple clients who were, by nature, savers. Growing up, we pick up on money traits our parents have, and apparently these clients' parents were frugal. In both cases, both spouses had good careers they cared about. The first couple knew that when kids came, the wife wanted to stay home to raise their children. Their high savings rate before kids made that an easy decision. The other spouses both kept working for several years. Then the wife found work less fulfilling as she realized how fast the kids were growing up. Being a big saver for years actually led her to worry that they would not be able to reach their goals if she quit her job. But seeing projections that showed she would have enough savings gave her the confidence to do what she wanted, not what she thought she had to do. It is hard to estimate the flexibility saving provides until you are in a situation where you need it.

The antidote to the danger of saving without a specific purpose is to instill some mechanism to prevent yourself from being mesmerized by numbers in your account. The goal is to find something to remind you—firmly and deeply—that only God is great. We've found that the best mechanism is a trusted friend who has permission to speak into your life. When that person finds you a little too focused on that new car or fancy watch, they can bring you back to the truth that God is great, not wealth or anything you could buy.

Calculating LIVE, GIVE, OWE, and GROW

A lot of people hate budgeting and tracking each expense, so they wind up not knowing where their money is going. Fortunately, categorizing your cash flow into these four categories allows you to get really close to knowing the breakdown using only your tax return (and perhaps a few other items depending on your situation).

Start by finding your total earnings for the year—your gross pay. If you are retired, this would be the total of portfolio withdrawals plus other income such as Social Security, pensions, rental property income, etc. We'll use Jim and Lorraine as our example. They are in their early sixties and have a combined income of $450,000.

Next, using your tax return, we will calculate what goes into the OWE category. Add the Federal, state, and real estate taxes. If you have a mortgage, the interest will be on your Schedule A if you itemize. If you have student loans, auto loans, or anything else you pay interest on, you will need to find those separately. Your goal is to know what you paid in taxes plus any interest you paid. For Jim and Lorraine, they paid $95,000 in income taxes and $15,000 in real estate taxes. They do not have any other debts, so their total for the OWE category is $110,000.

The GIVE category can also be found on Schedule A unless you did not itemize. Even if you did not itemize, you likely added up your charitable gifts to find out if itemizing was best for you, so hopefully you can still find it. Last year Jim and Lorraine had $75,000 of charitable gifts.

The GROW category is next and can be a little tricky to figure out. A W-2 should show you what you put into a 401(k) or 403(b). Also add in any other retirement contributions such as IRA or Roth IRA contributions. If you contributed to a 529 college savings account, you will add that in too. Finally, add in any other savings. This could be a monthly transfer into a savings account or just the accumulation in your checking account. A rough estimate is always fine; we aren't trying to dial in any category to an exact percentage. We just want to get a general view of where your dollars are going. Jim and Lorraine contributed $25,000 to their retirement plan and saved $15,000 in their taxable investment account for a total of $40,000.

To figure out the LIVE category, simply take the income you calculated in the first step and subtract everything else. For Jim and Lorraine, this is $450,000 minus $110,000 (OWE – 24%) minus $75,000 (GIVE – 17%) minus $40,000 (GROW – 9%) for a total of $225,000 in their LIVE category (50%).

If you did this exercise, are you surprised by the results? As we mentioned earlier, this is where the hard work is. Take time to reflect and consider what you would ideally like the breakdown to be. It is an endeavor worth taking and the reward of contentment cannot be oversold.

Default Financial Planning	Biblically & Purposefully
LIVE – Having money = spending money	LIVE – Steward what God has entrusted us with. Be content. Be humble.
GIVE – Give from what is left over after the other uses. Not much thought, purpose, or joy.	GIVE – Reflecting God's generosity to us, we give cheerfully and purposefully.
OWE – Debt is normal and the only way to live in the modern world.	OWE – Debt is warned against, depending on how it is used, and should not be used to fund lifestyle.
GROW – Two paths: one is living for today and doesn't save, the other believes what they accumulate will lead to happiness.	GROW – Need to know the purpose and not lose sight of the stewardship responsibility.

7

Getting Practical – Investing

IT'S MONDAY MORNING and the alarm clock rings. John slowly climbs out of bed. A few minutes later he hops on his exercise bike and turns on CNBC to catch up on what's moving the premarket trading. An hour later John heads to work, where he owns and operates a successful car dealership. Throughout the day he's checking his portfolio, and the highlight of his day is an email from an investment newsletter he subscribes to that has a list of buys and sells to consider. It was an up day for the markets, and that evening John impatiently waits to see the updated price of his investments so that he can see how much money he made that day. One day down; four more just like it await.

From the outside, John is a successful, driven man. On the inside, John is the epitome of discontentment. His mood and how he treats those around him is dictated by the success of the markets and his dealership. He sounds like a caricature of discontentment, but he is real.

Unfortunately, there are many, many more like him. Some are more extreme, others less, but they all have the same underlying tendencies. John embodies the Default Financial Planning mindset around investing. Let's unpack his actions one by one to reveal his underlying beliefs and how they are preventing him from reaching his goals while making him miserable.

The first thing we see is John's obsession with the financial media, which he follows because he thinks he will gain investment insights. The financial media's goal is to keep you entertained and watching. They've learned from The Weather Channel (TWC) that disasters equal viewers. TWC has an average of 150,000 prime time viewers during normal weather, but when natural disasters hit, viewership rises to over a million. TWC just has to wait for those natural disasters to occur, but as soon as they do advertisers are lined up ready to pay higher rates to get their ads in front of more viewers. Likewise, the financial media taps into fear and greed to create their own kind of natural disaster, making you think you'll miss out on some crucial information if you turn away.

Some people recognize the tactics being used by the financial media, but they still tune in for the advice. But there's a problem—it's not advice. Sure, the guests of the shows are giving their opinions of the direction the markets or individual stocks will go in the short run, but just because they have a platform does not make their prediction any better than yours or mine.[1] This also assumes that all investors are the same. While in general, all investors want to earn a return on their investments, the way investors go about investing very much depends on their personal situation. A retired woman living on her pension is going to invest much differently than a woman just beginning her career, but the "advice" coming from their television will never make that distinction. Would you take a prescription from a doctor you had never met? Taking investment advice from someone who doesn't know your situation can be just as foolish.

The next thing you may have noticed was John's excitement around the investment newsletter with the list of possible trades. John has divided his portfolio among various, highly rated professional managers, each using a different strategy. He also keeps 20% of his portfolio in an account that he manages through an app on his phone, mostly because he thinks he can get better returns than the professionals. He adjusts the amounts each manager has based upon their recent returns, but he dreams of one day managing the entire portfolio himself.

What John fails to recognize is that he is betting and gambling, not investing. Participating in the markets does not automatically make you an investor any more than strumming a D chord on a guitar makes you a musician.

Jim Paul was a very successful commodities trader—for a while. In his book *What I Learned Losing a Million Dollars*, he makes distinctions about how you are participating in the markets based on the behavioral characteristics you display. Investing is always associated with a long-term horizon while betting and gambling focus on the short-term. A bettor is interested in being right. John wants to be right; he wants to outperform the professionals (as well as his golfing buddies). A gambler is looking for entertainment. Being right or wrong also leads to an adrenaline rush. John is anticipating that rush as soon as he sees his newsletter with potential trades.

Proverbs 13:11 says, "Wealth gained hastily will dwindle, but whoever gathers little by little will increase it." This is a difficult principle to follow in our culture, but the experience of many families we work with confirms its truth. The reason it is difficult to follow in our culture is that we've been sold on instant gratification. Almost anything can show up at your door at the click of a button—even if you don't have the cash to pay for it today. You're told you deserve it and to "treat yourself." With that as the norm, investing "little by little" seems outdated. An opportunity comes along—a chance to "get in on the ground floor" or a promise of high returns that "investment professionals don't want you to know about." Greed will stealthily come in and convince you that you might miss out. We're very good at telling stories to convince ourselves of just about anything. Our friend John tells himself this story to rationalize such appealing promises: "At my dealership, when new car sales are down, I'm able to make up for it in my service department if I just put some pressure on my service manager. That just makes sense—it is diversification. Investing must be the same, and this investor I'm listening to seems like the kind of guy who knows how to put pressure where it's needed in his portfolio. How else would he be able to generate such high returns?" We all need to take Proverbs 13 to heart. None of us is above making a mistake by trying to get rich quick.

A well-known leader in the financial advisor world teaches us a valuable lesson on this point. He owns a company that serves advisors, has authored several books, is a prolific conference speaker, and has a column in one of the industry magazines. He has a trusted advisor of his own and is a man of faith who has surely read that proverb before. He was also conned out of nearly a million dollars and his mother lost her entire life savings to a fraudulent real estate developer (but the details of the fraud aren't relevant here). There are two lessons to be learned here: do not underestimate how the get-rich-quick mentality can penetrate your own investment strategy, and do not risk what you have for what you don't need. His mother risked all her investable assets, which she needed to sustain her quality of life, for high rates of return that she didn't need. Would her quality of life increase with those high returns? Sure, there might be some marginal improvement, but nothing comparable to the quality of life she lost. This man summarized the ordeal, saying, "Seeing my mother not be able to sleep well for years in what should be the peaceful twilight of life is a far worse consequence than seeing hard-earned money evaporate."[2]

> Do not risk what you have for what you don't need.

A Better Way

If John shows us what investing with discontentment looks like, what does investing with contentment look like? The following paragraphs outline how we advise clients after decades in the business. It isn't the only successful approach—you can easily find phenomenal track records of famous investors and plenty of anecdotal evidence of other approaches that have been successful. The approach we outline is simply what we believe in.

It all starts with *why*. What is the purpose for these dollars?[3] As we said in the last chapter, dollars going into the GROW category are best invested with a known and measurable purpose. Is it for the down payment on a home, college, or retirement? Each will require a different investment approach as they are vastly different needs. Knowing *why* is so important because it directly influences the amount of risk you are willing to take. There is much that can be said about how to balance stocks versus bonds (and perhaps other categories) in your portfolio, far beyond what we can cover here. The main point we want to make is that whatever blend of investments you choose, it needs to allow you to sleep at night. If you aren't comfortable with the investments when you first choose them, you will not be comfortable with them when the market goes through some rough patches.

We need to control our impulses around investments. There is a joke that says investments are like a bar of soap: the more you touch them, the smaller they get. It is good behavior to not touch them unnecessarily. We have found the best way to get people to behave appropriately with their investments is to connect them with the purpose they have stated. Consider the real estate scam—would you allow your mother to put funds she needs to live (a very clear purpose for the money) into high-risk investments? Probably not. In the same way, knowing the money is to be used 20 years from now can keep younger people from making a knee-jerk reaction to market news. Knowing the purpose makes the difference.

Here are three further principles that will help guide you on this better way:

Principle #1: Choose an investment strategy you can stick with.

Choosing a strategy you'll be comfortable with in good times and bad will save you a whole host of problems in the future.

The main reason it is so important is because of *compounding*. Compounding is an investor's best friend. Simply put, compounding is the money you have made in the past continuing to earn returns. They say that a diversified portfolio is the only free lunch in investing—meaning it is a way to improve your portfolio without any additional cost or effort. We think compounding is the way to future lunches for yourself and others—it's not totally free, but if you stick with your strategy in the good markets and bad it will pay off.

For a simple example, think about a savings account that pays 1% interest. If you have $100 in the account, after a year you will have $101. The next year you earn 1% on the entire $101 which leads to $1.01 the following year. It doesn't seem like all that big of a deal when we're looking at small amounts over a small period, but when it comes to your long-term savings, the impact of compounding cannot be overstated.

Perhaps our favorite example of the power of compounding is Warren Buffett. Buffett, the famous investor and CEO of Berkshire Hathaway, made 96% of his wealth after his 65th birthday.[4] This wasn't due to one great stock pick he made on his 65th birthday—rather, his investments compounded year after year so that the amount was huge towards the end.

The hardest part of this principle is not understanding compounding, but sticking with your strategy when the market is in a downward trend and you're watching your balances decline. We've been advising some clients long enough that they've gone through several major stock market declines, and some have stuck with it while others sold at the bottom. These are a few of the lessons we've learned:

There will always be something to worry about. Some issues turn out to be no big deal and the market continues higher. Sometimes the issues are a big deal and they do cause the market to decline. There is just no way of consistently knowing whether an issue turns out to be a big deal until after the decline.

We also learned the importance of education. It helps to know that, on average, one out of every four years the stock market will see a significant decline.[5] Unfortunately, the decline doesn't come on a set schedule like the Olympics, and we don't have any insight into the severity or length of the decline. It is your behavior during these declines that will determine much of your success. Stick with it—don't sell out.

You also need to know when you will make a change to your investments. It makes sense for most people to be aggressive when they are young and saving for retirement. It also intuitively makes sense that you don't want to remain that aggressive forever. We like to say that you shouldn't make changes to your investment strategy unless your life changes.

There are dozens of life transitions that could necessitate a change of strategy—a job loss, a large change to income, family changes (divorce, death, illness, disability), etc. It is appropriate to re-evaluate your investment strategy when such changes occur. There are also predetermined times to make changes like a planned retirement age. Plan for how that will change your investments and make changes according to that plan, not based on market conditions.

Before moving on to the next principle, it is worth noting here that your beliefs around money will affect how you accomplish this. Our clients who handle market downturns well tend to have a loose grip on their money, meaning they know that God has given them a responsibility with the resources in their control and that He is in ultimate control. They believe the best way to steward that money is to understand the economic principles we've discussed thus far (and those following below) and to trust God to provide even if the investments don't work out. The opposite view of money tends to have more difficulty with economic downturns and understandably so. If you associate your value and worth as a human being with the balance of your investment portfolio, market declines will have you desperately searching for a solution to stop the pain.

Principle #2: Own it all.

The first principle is much easier to follow if you own it all—meaning you own all available investments (or more commonly a representative selection) of an investment category rather than constantly searching for individual investments which are predicted to outperform all others. Consider US stocks as an example. If you dedicate a portion of your investment in US stocks, "owning it all" could mean owning an investment that mimics the Russell 3000, which is roughly 3,000 stocks that represent the entirety of the US market. As we mentioned earlier, there are many viable investment approaches—but there are three reasons why we believe in Principle #2:

1) the overwhelming evidence for the difficulty of outperforming the related index,
2) the potential cost savings, and

3) the increased ability to be content compared to a more active and hands-on approach.

Let's take a deeper look at each of these reasons.

The investment management industry is not new, yet the efficacy of the strategies which try to outperform the index has not exactly been improving. Perhaps the best illustration of this is a study that is done each year by Dimensional Fund Advisors called the Mutual Fund Landscape. The study looks at all mutual funds each year, tracking the performance of each and determining if they were able to outperform their benchmark. What they find is that most managers cannot outperform their benchmarks after costs. You may think that you could pick the managers who have proven themselves to be able to outperform. The study highlights that remaining a top performer is difficult. About 1 in 4 managers can outperform over a 10-year period, and only 1 in 5 of those repeat that performance in the next 5-year period.[5] Investing always involves risk, but the risk-return profile for using active mutual fund managers that try to outperform the market seems like a poor bet, especially when you consider the added cost.

According to Investopedia,[6] investments that actively seek to outperform the index cost 0.61% more than investments that seek to simply own a representation of the market segment they are in. Let's be even more generous and assume it is only a 0.50% cost increase per year and look at the impact over time. Let's assume you are saving $500 per month over a 40-year career, with an 8% return each year. That will grow to $1,764,295. However, if you only earn 7.5% each year because of investment costs, that would grow to only $1,526,348.[6] It's still a large amount, but significantly less. Don't make the mistake of thinking that "you get what you pay for." While that is often true with things like home repair and travel, the world of investing is full of strange and counterintuitive facts.

Another reason we believe in principle #2 is that it helps with both contentment and stewardship. When your investment strategy is to own it all, you know that you'll essentially get what the market return is, adjusted for the blend of stocks and bonds you chose. You are freed from reviewing investment managers, looking at market forecasts, studying interest rates and market cycles, considering sector rotation, and on and on. Participating in those chores can quickly throw fuel on the discontentment fire. Why is this manager underperforming? Did I miss a chance at buying that stock while it was cheap? Why didn't I buy (insert hot investment) before it went on this run? It was so obvious! It is difficult not to fall into that line of thinking.

And then there is the time stewardship aspect. Is it a good use of your time to study the market questions outlined in the previous paragraph? We've already given some statistics showing the difficulty of improving investment returns beyond what the market does as a whole, and that is another big hurdle that many overlook: to "beat the market" you have to be "smarter" than professional investors. Professional investors have all sorts of tools to access information that you will never have and a lot more time than you do to make sense of it all. Think back to John and the 20% of his portfolio he is trying to outperform with. What this means is that he believes he can spend an hour or two a day and outperform his investment managers, who have teams of dozens of highly and well-educated financial analysts each spending 60 hours a week on research.

The reason so many try to do this highlights another strange fact of finance: regular Joes can and do sometimes outperform the professionals. Think about it: you can have no experience at all and do better than those who do this for a living. Where else does this occur? No one has car problems and thinks, "I'll read an article about transmissions and then I'll be able to fix mine and it will be better than the guys at the neighborhood garage." The big problem with investing is that you can get away with that strategy for a while, and maybe even do quite well, but a time will come when it all catches up with you. Unfortunately, it usually comes out of the blue and is devasting to your personal finances.

Several years ago, one of Eric's children became ill. It wasn't life threatening, but it did require several nights in the hospital. When the issue first became apparent, Eric's first reaction wasn't to check out WebMD—he went to their doctor and then the experts at the children's hospital. There are times when we do some research on our own and there are times when we recognize that we need an expert. Let's not be WebMD investors. Take that time back, be with your family, get some exercise, do anything except researching investment ideas that you think will help you outperform the broad market.

Principle #3: Manage your emotions.

In 1949, Benjamin Graham wrote what is probably the most famous book on investing, *The Intelligent Investor*. In it he says, "the investor's chief problem—and even his worst enemy—is likely to be himself." Seventy-plus years later, this is a still problem that plagues investors. We hear a story on the news, and it makes us worried. Then we look at our investment portfolio and see that our investments are reflecting this bad news. Repeat this over a few days and weeks and now our portfolios are much lower than they were. Now we're stressed out and constantly checking the balances in hopes that things turn around. Eventually we hit a tipping point and we act. We sell some of our stocks and we feel relief—for a moment. Inevitably, the market begins to go back up. Is now the time to get back in? The news is still bad. We wait. Stocks go higher and higher. Our stress goes higher and higher. This is a terrible roller coaster. Author and *New York Times* columnist Carl Richards captures this typical behavior in a simple sketch:

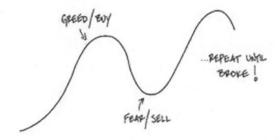

We're comfortable buying when times are good, and we want out when times get tough. This is a normal response, but devastating to an investment portfolio. What is the solution?

There is no magic bullet that will fix this issue because the up-and-down of the market is the price of admission for market returns. Without it you can't have the long-term market return of 10.5%.[8] To fully reduce risk, you would have to go with something like the 1-month treasury note with a long-term return of 3.3% (adjusted for inflation, this becomes 0.3%).[9] We show these rates of returns to help you see that, unless you have an unbelievably high savings rate, you'll need to take on at least some market risk to meet your objectives. Knowing that you must endure some of the up and down of the market, remember the following things to help alleviate the stress when the market takes a turn for the worse.

First, remember the principles that we started with. Don't interrupt the compounding of your investments unnecessarily. If you make a change to your strategy based on what is happening in the world, you are interrupting the compounding! Next, remember why you own it all—it's because you believe it is the best option available. Investor Warren Buffett is famous for investing in the exact opposite way, yet even he says, "In my view, for most people, the best thing to do is own the S&P 500 index fund."[10] When he says "index fund" you should hear "own it all." Buffett is acknowledging that the investment world has changed for the average investor. It's much like what happened with Blockbuster Video. To watch a movie at home you used to have to go across town to the local Blockbuster and walk the aisles to find something that caught your eye. Technology has advanced and now you can watch any movie you want on one of the streaming services. Similarly, there was a time when you went to a stockbroker to purchase individual companies or receive recommendations for an investment manager. Perhaps you remember doing this yourself! Times have changed and technology has advanced, and investing has changed just like movie rentals.

During market volatility, you would do well to review these principles and stay away from the financial media, lest you become convinced the hurricane is approaching and the only option you have is to sell, sell, sell!

Conclusion

A lot has been said, but a lot more could be said. Be sure to check out our recommended reading at the back of the book for more. For now, it really comes down to which approach you will take.

Will you take the difficult path of trying to outwork and outsmart the market—a path that takes outsized risks in the hopes of significant gains and allows market conditions and returns to influence your emotions? Or will you take the path that emphasizes stewardship of your time and contentment in the things outside of your control—a path that is also academically and historically sound and takes advantage of the power of compounding?

Default Financial Planning	Biblically & Purposefully
More effort = higher returns.	Better off owning it all because (1) the data and logic backs this and (2) this allows us to be better stewards of our time, spending it on things that matter.
Find a good professional who outperforms.	Nothing stays the same long. Don't be enticed by past performance or back-tested strategies
Know when to protect and when to be aggressive.	Fear and greed, while common in investing, can ruin investment returns
Investments are meant to make me rich.	Start with your *why* to determine the appropriate blend of investments.
Bigger portfolio = time for more "advanced" investing techniques.	"Own it all" is sufficient. "Advanced" is generally code for high fees and likely playing off of fear or greed. Contentment allows us to ignore such ploys.

8

Getting Practical – Retirement

IN MAY OF 2000, John Piper gave what would become one of the first viral sermons of the internet age. The introduction is so memorable that it became the nickname for the sermon: "The Seashell Sermon."

Piper tells the story of a couple who retired when he was 59 and she was 51. They moved to Florida where they cruised on their thirty-foot trawler, played softball, and collected shells. Piper pleads with the crowd that this is the wrong dream to follow—there is something better for them. He ends the introduction imagining this couple before God giving an account for their life and saying "Here it is, Lord—my shell collection! And I've got a nice swing, and look at my boat!"

It's humorous and memorable, meant to drive home a point. The point is that we are called to far more than simply living for the good life. When did the overwhelming consensus become that the focus of every worker should be retirement as soon as possible? To help answer that, we must take a quick trip back to before retirement was even a concept.

The history of retirement in America is a fascinating story. Early on, retirement as we know it did not exist. If you were alive, you worked—and probably on a farm. It wasn't until industrialization that retirement became a concept. Prior to that, there were pensions for some—mostly veterans or firefighters—but it was rare. To increase production, the older workers were replaced by younger workers, which broadened the idea of retirement to nearly everyone as they got older.

The first government to create a retirement system was Germany in the 1880s. That system provided for citizens once they were 70 years old. At that time, life expectancy was not yet 50 years. In the United States, American Express was offering private pensions and certain industries like railroads, oil, and banking were also providing benefits to those who couldn't work any longer. But it wasn't until the Great Depression that the US government followed Germany's lead and started the public pension. FDR and his New Deal brought about the Social Security Administration in 1935. They pegged retirement at age 65, purely for economic reasons. The life expectancy at the time? Late 50s or early 60s. The program was criticized for a couple of reasons. First, very few lived long enough to claim any benefits and then second, those getting benefits were still living in poverty. This is still a far cry from the view of retirement today.

World War II played an important role in the evolution of retirement in America. Wages were frozen so businesses began to use pensions to further compensate employees. The combination of these pensions along with Social Security payments led to respectable retirements. Significant advancements in safety and medicine also meant that people were finally living long enough to collect benefits.

While the increase in life expectancy might seem like the reason for the change in retirement, it really comes down to the fact that World War II essentially created the middle class. We won't get into details, but consider that the average American's disposable income rose nearly 75% between 1929 and 1950.[1] The middle class emerged, and the economy shifted its focus from military spending to consumer spending. The postwar consumerism created new demand for financial products and services. Retirement was now being marketed as the rightful reward for years of labor and loyal service. A new mentality was born.

This mentality has evolved some over the years but remains at the heart of how most people view retirement today.

The Default Position

We once saw a mug that read "Strategic Retirement Plan: 1. Rest. 2. Relax. 3. Repeat." This is the post-WWII American retirement dream.

Most people are doing all they can to obtain that dream sooner rather than later. We have seen this default mentality play out in many times, but the one that stands out is Jonathan's story.

Jonathan was a diligent saver throughout his career, motivated entirely by how soon he could retire. All his money moves were textbook examples. He never took unnecessary risks, and he kept his funds invested even during economic turmoil when others would be tempted to abandon their plan. Unfortunately, textbook financial moves often come with a personal cost. Jonathan worked long hours away from his family. Vacations were rare and stressful—he did not like being away from the office or spending extra money. What he did like were the weekends—a couple of days to recharge his batteries and do whatever he pleased.

Weekends are a good thing, and we know this because God gave us the Sabbath as a day to rest each week. The problem is that the default position twists this gift. People begin to work for the weekend because it represents freedom—doing what you want to do when you want to do it. Retirement, then, is seen as complete freedom, not just the temporary freedom of the weekends. Every night is Friday night, and every day is Saturday. This is so deeply ingrained in our society that telling someone you aren't planning for a traditional retirement will generate strange looks, much like what Noah must have gotten while building the ark. The problem is that we know that the life of pure leisure leads to a flood of boredom and emptiness.

> The problem is that we know that the life of pure leisure leads to a flood of boredom and emptiness.

Consider what we learned back in chapter 5: work is the God-ordained means for contributing to society, finding fulfillment, and meeting material needs so we can provide for our families. If rest and relaxation take the place of work, where is contribution to society? Can a life of leisure bring us fulfillment?

Contrast Jonathan with Linda. She had been working with our firm since before either of us had begun our careers. In one of our first meetings, we brought up her plan for retirement (at this point we still believed in the default view of retirement and were about to get our first glimpse at a better way). Linda had more money than she needed to live a comfortable life in retirement, yet she was still working. This didn't make sense to us— didn't she want to leave the pressures of the business world and start her life of freedom? When we asked why she kept working, she told us that not only did she enjoy working, but since she had more money than she needed, working allowed her to support causes that she deeply cared about.

Linda understood that just because she had reached a certain age and level of financial security did not mean that she lost the purpose of her life. Rather, she was able to be even more intentional since she knew what enough was for her. She had set a financial finish line and, once she crossed it, decided not to rest and relax but to use her business skills to bless others. Linda was able to do this, in part, because she enjoyed her work. What about those who don't enjoy their work?

When you understand your purpose for work, this will be far easier to figure out. It will be different for everyone; there is no right or wrong as long as you frame the question correctly. We've had some clients who worked in the corporate world and then shifted to working for a non-profit they care about. This requires planning and an idea of what you want life to look like as you get older. What we can say with certainty is that putting in 30–40 years at a job you can't stand just to save as much as you can so you can retire to a life of leisure is not going to pay off the way you expect.

Studies show that a significant percentage of people are dissatisfied with their jobs. Unfortunately, many of those people have bought into the default view that retirement is the solution to this problem. They believe that once they retire, they'll lose the cause of their grief and they'll gain the freedom to do all the things they want to do—rest, relax, repeat. That belief is understandable. It's not just coffee mugs telling them this. Corporate America has been structured around this idea. Entire industries exist around this premise, from elaborately planned retirement communities to our own industry of wealth management.

Going back to Jonathan, he found his work to be frustrating and often questioned the effort he was putting in. Decades of making that effort was exhausting, so, when he was 58, Jonathan decided to retire. It was finally time to get the reward he deserved for years of hard work.

What Jonathan didn't realize was that the discontentment he felt in work would continue in retirement. We saw earlier that true contentment comes from within ourselves and not external sources. It comes from joyfully resting in God's providence. If we don't have it while we are laboring, we cannot expect it to come when we are not laboring. Jonathan was soon going to find out that the discontentment he felt in his work would be replaced with discontentment in his retirement along with lost identity, boredom, and emptiness.

Retire with Purpose

Family Feud is a game show in which contestants try to guess the most common answers from a survey of 100 people (could we really write a chapter about retirement and not mention game shows?). One survey question asked people to name an activity that is associated with retired people. The most common responses were golf, bingo, cards, fishing, shuffleboard, and travel. If you were looking for a list that described the generic view of the retirement lifestyle, there it is. Notice that it is full of leisure activities.

When we retire, we are expected to enter a life of leisure—nothing but rest and relaxation.

But this idea of retirement is flawed. Leisure is only enjoyable when it is rest from work. Without the work, leisure becomes less and less effective. We need work and purpose in our lives.

We were in contact quite a bit with Jonathan leading up to his retirement, but once he retired,

> Leisure is enjoyable when it is rest from work.

we didn't hear from him for months. We figured he was busy enjoying his retirement and didn't feel the need to check in. We knew he enjoyed golf and had family and friends he would spend time with. We figured he was living the typical retirement life.

After a few months we heard from Jonathan. We asked how it was going and he said that it was actually turning out to be a difficult adjustment. He had spent the last few months trying to figure it out. A couple of weeks later we heard from him again. The next call followed soon after, and the next even sooner. Jonathan was realizing he had bought into a flawed view of retirement. He had prioritized saving for retirement over time with family, vacations, and other passions in pursuit of a life he realized he didn't want.

There were three common struggles in these calls, which we alluded to earlier, and they are worth looking at in more detail as they are common among those who realize that pure leisure is not all that it is hyped up to be.

Many people who retire to a life of leisure will struggle with *identity*. Jonathan was no exception. Having climbed the corporate ladder, he was used to making big decisions and having the respect of his coworkers. If our identity is not in Christ, we will often find our identity in our work and the role that we held at work. This is especially true for those who, like Jonathan, were in an authoritative position (C-suite executives, attorneys, coaches, etc.).

Boredom is also a significant issue. Many will go back to work in some way, not for the money but to break up the monotony of constant leisure. They've spent their careers climbing a ladder, but at the top they realized it was leaning against the wrong building. They didn't really want a life of pure leisure. What they wanted was a job that brought them satisfaction. Others will find new pursuits and interests to fill the boredom. For Jonathan, he began focusing on his investments. Part of our phone calls involved him asking questions about recent activity he had seen on his accounts. He had never cared about this before, but now it gave him something to do and satisfaction in completing a task each day.

Lastly, there is *emptiness* found in a life of leisure. Many people early in their retirement wonder, "Is this it? Is this really what I worked so hard for?" Sometimes the things their 30-year-old selves thought they would do in retirement are no longer interesting in their retirement years. Sometimes people will say they want to travel in their retirement only to find their health and energy has declined and they wish they had done the traveling earlier. Whatever the cause, the emptiness highlights the importance of understanding who we are, what we are called to, how to steward what God has entrusted us with, and how to do all of this with contentment—trusting in God's providence.

Before they retire, many people will spend hours upon hours examining their retirement plan, investments, withdrawal rates, and what-if scenarios, yet spend very little time thinking about how they will invest their time and energy once retired. Retired people still have responsibility to steward their time well. Often it seems that people think stewardship of their time stops when their paycheck ends. This is not the case at all! Now that you have more time, you need to decide how to use it. What will you do to avoid boredom? Will you consult part-time or volunteer with a local non-profit? What will you do to

> You need to retire *to* something and not *from* your job.

bring purpose to your life? Will you teach Sunday School or share your wisdom with your grandchildren?

Linda is a good example of retiring with purpose. Linda retired later than the traditional retirement age but found herself wanting a slower pace. Even for those who don't desire to retire as early as possible, there will still come a time when moving to a slower pace is right and good. She cut back her hours over a couple of years before fully retiring. When she retired, however, she did not retire to a life of leisure.

We often say that you need to retire *to* something and not just *from* your job. Simply retiring from work puts you at a very high risk of falling into the issues we just looked at. Linda retired to volunteering with her church and several local non-profits as well as spending a lot of time with family and friends. These things kept her active and engaged. She also spent time doing other activities that made the Family Feud list, but they were not the main objective of her retirement. When that balance is kept, you can truly enjoy those activities as good gifts. They become problematic when they are the sole focus.

Linda's retirement worked out just as she had imagined it, but usually we see clients go through unexpected challenges during retirement—a spouse falling ill or premature death is most common. Perhaps you start caring for grandchildren. We have seen that our clients who are content in the role God has called them to in retirement, whether an elder at their church or homebound due to illness, can thrive despite any circumstances.

Conclusion

Up to this point we have been very practical about retirement, but there are some deeper issues to consider. Many of these issues require wisdom and discernment because they are in tension with others. Just like no two budgets are exactly alike, no two retirement plans should be exactly alike either. God gives us the freedom to make these decisions for ourselves and we should approach them with an appropriate level of seriousness.

> We hoard money because we fear what will happen if we do not have enough.

Consider how much to save for retirement. In the cash flow chapter, we did not give a recommended amount to save. Instead, we emphasized the need to find a balance among the four ways to use money (OWE, GROW, LIVE, and GIVE). Even if we narrow the GROW category to just retirement, the balance will still be unique to each person.

Each person needs to find a balance between saving enough for retirement and not neglecting the other categories. In Proverbs 6 we are told to be wise like the ant who prepares for harvest rather than lazy like the sluggard. The ant and sluggard are polar opposites—black and white. How much to save in retirement is a shade of gray. We ought to save enough to allow for flexibility, since life is full of unexpected events that could drain our funds. We also don't want to be a burden to others—Proverbs 21 tells us a foolish man devours what he has

> It is hard to meaningfully pray to God asking for our daily bread if our barns are so full that it would take a cataclysmic event to be in need.

and leaves nothing stored for the future. Yet we also ought not save too much for retirement, lest we trust in our money rather than trusting God.

For many of us, it is far too easy to trust in money rather than God. We hoard money because we fear what will happen if we don't have enough. This is another reason we would do well to have a trusted friend who knows our heart and situation well to talk this through with. We can't guard against every possible risk, but it would be foolish to not guard against *any* risks. We should have some safety margin in our retirement savings, but how much is too much? It is hard to meaningfully pray for our daily bread if our barns are so full that it would take a cataclysmic event to be in need. In the parable of the rich man, God called the rich man a fool for the way he hoarded his wealth—he was rich toward himself and not toward God.

Can you feel the tension? We can handle these difficulties best by focusing on our roles as stewards. God owns it all—we have no rights, just responsibilities. It is our responsibility to look at how much we are saving and determine how much is enough. We do not want to be the rich fool, yet we also don't want to be the sluggard who asks God to take care of it all while we do nothing. We are responsible to find that balance for ourselves.

The job of a steward does not end with finding that balance. We are then responsible for the legacy we leave. That is where we will turn next. We want to finish well, leaving both a financial and spiritual legacy for the next generation.

Default Financial Planning	Biblically & Purposefully
Work is frustrating, exhausting and controls me – the sooner it is over the better!	We all have a calling and purpose in our lives and that is not in conflict with meaningful work.
Retirement is all about leisure – rest, relax, repeat.	True contentment is often found in the balance of good things.
Save as much as you can so that you can retire as early as you can.	A balance must be found in cash flow and saving. It is possible to save too much.
Retire to get away from work.	Retire *to* something, not just *from* your job.

9

Getting Practical – Legacy

THERE ARE 2,930 people mentioned in the Bible. Many of them we don't know much about, but have a fuller picture of about 100 of them. Of these 100, only about one third of them finished well.[1] Finishing well was rare then, and it is rare now. We all *want* to finish well, so what can be done to make that a reality? There are many areas of our lives in which we can fail to finish well, but perhaps none is as common as areas related to wealth.

Proverbs 11:28 tells us that those who trust in their wealth will fall. Those who trust in their wealth will not finish well. Throughout this book we have emphasized that God owns it all, and that we must be content and good stewards of what He entrusts us. If that message has taken root, you may be tempted to look past this warning. However, the passage says that those who trust in their wealth will fall—it does not say that if you refrain from trusting in wealth you will succeed. There are still many ways that believers with wealth can go wrong even if they trust in God, especially when it comes to what to do with that wealth as they age.

Two Legacies

The last chapter ended with figuring out how much is enough— finding the balance between hoarding wealth (trusting in it rather than God) and being a sluggard (who expects God to take care of it all while doing nothing for himself). Having figured this out, we must next make plans for our wealth for when we are gone. And being good stewards, we know that this is something that must be done now and not put off for another day.

When most people think about this sort of planning, they think about estate planning (decisions about what will happen to their financial assets). As believers, we ought to be thinking about legacy planning, which consists of two components: spiritual and financial. The spiritual and financial legacies we leave are deeply intertwined, and we believe that no Christian should leave a financial legacy without first addressing the spiritual legacy.

Before we look deeper at these two legacies we will leave, let's first look at the default legacy-leaving process.

The Default

Margaret and her husband, Robert, had worked hard for years and built a successful specialty manufacturing business while also raising three children. When she was in her late 60s, Margaret received an offer to sell the family business to a much larger company. Robert had passed away 3 years earlier, and Margaret no longer enjoyed running the business even though her son, David, had moved up from his accounting role to fill his dad's shoes. Margaret decided to sell, despite David's desire to keep the business, figuring that the money her children would eventually receive would make up for any hard feelings.

The other two children—a son with a rebellious streak who had trouble holding down a job and a daughter who was married with a family of her own—were both hoping the sale would lead to some immediate financial help. Margaret helped them from time to time, but always with strings attached that caused tension in the family.

A few years later Margaret passed away, and her children gathered for the reading of the will. None of them had any knowledge of their mother's plans. David, having worked in the business most of his life, was given half of the estate outright. The other two children received a quarter of the estate in a trust, with David as the trustee. This reality hit while they were still processing losing their mother. How do you think it went over? Do you think it brought the family together or caused additional friction?

In Margaret's defense, she had created her estate plan after selling the business and was trying to be fair with the effort David had put into it. She had concerns about the other children's ability to handle the newfound wealth and the trust seemed like the only logical choice to protect them from bad choices.

Margaret's decisions align with the default view of estate planning:

1. This money is mine and I have every right to decide how it is used while when I'm here and when I'm gone.
2. I will decide what is fair.
3. These plans are private; after all, I may need to change them!

These views, while common, are not the way a steward ought to think about estate planning. We also know there is more to be done than simply creating a plan for distribution of our financial assets. We have a legacy to create.

Creating Legacies

Spiritual

Perhaps you find yourself in a position similar to Margaret. Maybe you built a business and realize you have wealth you need to steward well, or perhaps after years of monthly savings you find yourself in that same situation. Regardless of how you got there, you are feeling the burden of finishing well and stewarding this wealth. The goal for the remainder of this chapter is to equip and encourage you to bring purpose to these decisions while avoiding planning by default.

Epictetus, the Greek Stoic philosopher, advised, "Be careful to leave your sons well instructed rather than rich, for the hopes of the instructed are better than the wealth of the ignorant."[2] While the instruction we have in view here is different, the principle is the same. Without instruction, an inheritance is not of much value. Our culture tells us otherwise, advocating the myth that wealth brings happiness. There is perhaps no greater demonstration of this myth than the book *The Legacy of Inherited Wealth* by Katherine Gibson and Margaret Kiersted. The authors interviewed many people who had inherited enough money that they no longer had to work. They wrote, "If there is one accurate generalization we can draw from these interviews, it is that abundant wealth has a way of separating heirs from the grist of life. For some inheritors, this separation manifests as a painful inability to identify their real needs and longings. . . . Other heirs find it difficult to establish authentic and trusting friendships; they worry that perhaps their net worth matters more to friends than their self-worth. Still others find it hard to connect with meaningful work."

Clearly this is not what people have in mind when drafting their estate plans. But it doesn't have to be that way. The authors noted that for some heirs who were "well prepared to receive family money," it turned out well. You can prepare your heirs by first passing along your values then the wisdom on how to handle money biblically before passing along any dollars. Leaving a spiritual legacy will be a concern for any serious disciple of Jesus. Our treatment of the issue is not to provide instruction on how to leave a legacy, but rather a reminder that it is a top priority. This is not to say that you should not leave any inheritance to a non-believer, but we want to consider the wisdom of doing so. Is it good stewardship to leave funds you know will not be used for biblical purposes?

When it comes to teaching the next generation how to handle money biblically, the reality is that more will be "caught" than "taught." You must model this for them. It is hard work, but it is a responsibility that cannot be deferred to another or ignored without consequence. Our favorite example of this comes from the founder of our firm, Ruth Guillaume. Ruth and her husband, Stan, have a tradition with their grandchildren where they give each of them $100 at Thanksgiving and charge them with figuring out how they will use that money to help others. Then, at Christmas, the children must share with them how it was used and why. They could give to an organization, a person they knew in need, or anyone else as long the purpose is to help others. This tradition gave them so many wonderful opportunities to learn the hearts of their grandchildren as well as to share their own hearts about who they are generous with and why.

It requires more than teaching and modeling generosity to pass down a biblical understanding of money; it encompasses everything we've covered in this book—living like God owns it all; sharing a proper view of work, cash flow, and spending choices; making decisions about stewardship of time; and prioritizing service to the kingdom. In these ways you can pass down wisdom prior to an inheritance. That is exactly what the writer of Ecclesiastes had in mind when he said, "Wisdom is good with an inheritance, an advantage to those who see the sun. For the protection of wisdom is like the protection of money, and the advantage of knowledge is that wisdom preserves the life of him who has it" (7:11-12). As Ron Blue says, "We need to prepare the kids for the money and not just prepare the money for the kids." The default is to focus on the money, buying into that myth that money will bring our heirs happiness. We must do better and focus on our spiritual legacy first. Once we do that, we can look at our financial legacy.

Financial

When leaving a financial legacy, people commonly make the mistake of focusing too much on what others will think of them when they are gone. Instead, the primary concern should be what God thinks of us. Our motivation should not be to keep our heirs happy so they say nice things about us. Our motivation should be to honor God with our final stewardship responsibilities.

We are first responsible for selecting our heirs, which we covered in the previous section. The typical next decision is how much to leave each heir, and how much to leave to charity. We saw how Margaret was influenced by the default view when trying to decide what was fair. We want to push back against these assumptions you might have by default.

> If we are not being intentional with our lifestyles, something will always catch our eye.

Let us start by stating that there is no universal way to do this, and it will be highly personalized with adjustments for unique family circumstances (health, age, etc.). We have a responsibility to our young families, so our plans will look vastly different than some of our clients in their 70s, 80s, and 90s.

That said, let's continue looking at someone in a situation like Margaret. If you are following our advice, you have figured out what enough is. We believe that excess money beyond your enough should be given away while you are alive and not as a part of your estate plan. We will expand on this belief, but a word about enough needs to start the discussion.

Because we are all human, we will need to fight the tendency to simply raise our standard of living up to what our portfolio can support such that we always have enough but nothing in excess of enough. If we are not being intentional with our lifestyles, something new will always cause the goalposts to move—so we end up adjusting our lifestyles whenever there is excess. This can happen very subtly, but we must be alert to this tendency if we are to be good stewards and content in what we have.

What *enough* is for you will change as you age, but ideally not because your lifestyle choices change. The amount of flexibility, cushion, or *enough* needed will be vastly different for a 60-year-old than for an 85-year-old. The 60-year-old may be far more active and traveling, while the 85-year-old may have significant healthcare expenses. However, it is not the level of expenses that are important here, but the number of years that the portfolio must last. Simply put, if you are 85 and have funds to last you 30 more years at your current living expenses, you have a great opportunity to, again quoting Ron Blue, "do your givin' while you're livin' so you're knowin' where it's goin.'"[3]

Why do we recommend giving away what is beyond your enough while still living?

To start, giving breaks the power of money over us (as we discussed in chapter 6), and since it is difficult to finish well, we ought to be particularly concerned about this when our portfolios are likely to be the largest. Giving will help prevent us from falling into the many traps that can come from wealth.

We also spent a fair amount of time in chapter 6 discussing the joy of giving. There is an additional joy available later in life when your giving is also a part of modeling a generous life for the next generation. Sometimes giving is viewed as a duty rather than a delight. We have yet to see anything but joy from those who invite others along on their giving journey.

The second part to the Ron Blue quote above is "so you're knowin' where it's goin.'" You might have heard the argument that gifts made after your death are of lesser eternal value because you did not choose to give the money away, it just happens to everyone when they die. The logic makes sense, but perhaps more persuasive arguments are that you can have the joy of seeing the fruits of the gifts and you can have greater confidence in the appropriate uses of your gifts. Mission drift is real and is an issue for those saving their giving for after their death. Consider the number of colleges that were once Christ-centered and now have abandoned those convictions. Or the churches and denominations that no longer hold to biblical orthodoxy. These risks can be avoided by doing your giving while living so that you know exactly where the money is going.

Another reason we recommend giving what is above your enough is that we acknowledge what large inheritances can do to your heirs. With advice like this it is easy to think that could only happen to other people. It's kind of like asking someone if they are an above-average driver. Everyone believes they are. And no one believes a significant inheritance will be harmful to their children. The stories of inherited wealth tell us otherwise—less desire for education, a refusal to grow up and take on responsibility, guilt, hoarding of wealth, etc. We should not be surprised by this possibility. Consider your own life and when you developed your character, work ethic, and discipline. For most, this comes when we have little to our name. Large inheritances will impact that development.

Perhaps you are thinking that by the time your children receive their inheritance they will likely be adults with a fully developed character. However, if your children are fully grown, it is not likely that they will need financial assistance (assuming, for example, that you pass around age 80 and your children are around age 50). We would argue that if they don't need the money, then it is not good stewardship on your part to give them what they don't need. If there is a true need, then absolutely you should provide. Sometimes parents can be hesitant to help one child without also making provisions for others. Ron Blue also has sage wisdom in this arena, teaching that we are to "love our children equally and as such treat them uniquely."[3] This can be a crucial aspect to leaving the kind of legacy you desire, but must be done with openness, as we discuss below.

You could also give this help during your lifetime as you try to model a biblical use of money. There is always a risk of creating an unhealthy dependence (i.e., are they spending it lavishly in a way that is incommensurate with their income?), so our advice is to be prayerful in how this support is given and to be aware of meeting needs versus funding lifestyle.

Perhaps you desire to abide by Proverbs 13:22 which says, "A good man leaves an inheritance to his children's children." But we must consider the context in which it was written. It is likely that this is referring to passing on ownership of land since during Old Testament times there were inheritance laws that allowed for the continuity of the family line. The inheritance was meant to maintain the family at a time when many lived at a subsistence level and without land could end up enslaved.[4]

Final Thoughts

Before we realized that we were simply helping clients "build bigger barns," we often helped them plan for large inheritances and considered our jobs well done when the numbers got bigger and bigger. But when we realized that the wealth we were helping clients build could be keeping them from knowing Christ, we changed how we gave advice, including about inheritances. Just as we cannot assist clients build bigger barns without asking why, we cannot build plans that leave large inheritances without also asking why.

We want to be clear that we do not think you should leave no inheritance at all. We want to encourage you to think of it instead in terms of a legacy. Stewarding what God has entrusted you with should be the goal. And whatever you decide to do, our encouragement is to be open with your family about your plans.

We have met with children who, completely unaware of their parent's situation or desires before they died, felt betrayed that they were not trusted with this knowledge and could not ask them why they made the choices they had made. Your goal should be to share appropriately so that there are not any mismatched expectations and can explain your desires. Use this as a time to build your legacy. If you are leaving them funds, consider giving them a test run by giving them some now. Watch how they manage it. Come alongside them when needed and teach them how to handle money biblically.

Jesus tells us to lay up treasures in heaven. The things we have on earth will perish, but what we do for the kingdom will not.[5] We do not know how much time we have until we will see those treasures, but we do know that the time will come. Given that uncertainty, you would do well to make your plans now—plans to leave a legacy, both spiritual and financial.

Default Financial Planning	Biblically & Purposefully
Estate planning documents are my last chance to get things done how I'd like.	We should be stewards with our last responsibility.
Estate planning documents are private.	Have honest and open conversations to share your wishes and heart.
Leaving my estate to my children is my legacy.	My legacy should be spiritual and then financial.
I need to treat my children equally.	We must love equally, but there is wisdom and prudence in treating individuals uniquely.

Conclusion

OUR HOPE IS that this book has been faithful to what the Bible teaches about money and that we have shown ways in which you can grow in your contentment and generosity as you steward what God has blessed you with. We encourage you to move beyond living by default and begin to bring purpose to your financial decisions. The default is easy, so expect this to be challenging. We pray that as you align the purpose of your finances with God's Word, you, your family, and the kingdom will be richly blessed.

What's Next?

Financial planning is a continuous process. It is not something you do once and then move on to the next thing. Similarly, this book is not something you can finish reading and then leave on the shelf. We're called to be stewards of our finances and that is not something we will ever get to check off as "completed." At different life stages there will be different challenges and opportunities to work through. To help illustrate how unique this can be, we thought it would be fitting for each of us to share how we have been implementing these principles in our lives.

Eric's Application

Ruth Guillaume hired me directly after graduation from Taylor University in July 2000. I interviewed at other Wall Street firms whose names you would recognize, and they tried to sell me on all they had to offer. This included money, status, more money, and working in a fancy downtown office. Ruth did not offer me any of that, but I knew she loved Jesus and cared for the clients she was serving. She offered me the opportunity to come alongside her and work in her growing business. The opportunity to work with someone like Ruth was appealing, and looking back I know it was God directing my steps. I am so thankful for the opportunity to work with Ruth. We continue to be friends and even, recently, next door neighbors.

The groundwork for this book was laid in 2006 when Colin Smith asked me to give a brief talk on contentment to some young preachers he was mentoring. I am still not sure why he asked me, but I started to read Puritan books (see the further reading recommendations for chapter 1). God started to work in my heart, and I desired to have discussions with clients about contentment and generosity. My faith and convictions started to have a meaningful impact on the work I was doing with clients. I wanted to offer clients advice based on what the Bible has to say. My view shifted from being a financial planner who was a Christian to a Christian financial planner—the difference is subtle but important. The world does not have the answers and those looking for financial planning advice are often looking for the certainty that only Jesus can provide.

These concepts also started to play out in my personal life. Right now, in Spring 2023, Jen and I have been married for 20 years and have four kids: Olivia is 14, Josiah is 12, Cade is 9, and Kaylee is 6. In 2014 we purchased land with the hopes of building our dream home. Building a new home is not the most cost-effective way to buy a house, and we were faced with many decisions concerning generosity, contentment, and long-term planning. The exact same things I was talking with clients about had to be applied to my own life. We wrestled with questions about how much we wanted to spend, what type of house would best suit our family, what priorities we wanted to focus on, and more. Were we okay with writing a check for 2x4's and shingles and less to kingdom ministries for a season? Building this house would delay retirement and limit immediate charitable giving, but we were convinced it was the path God had for us. We worked to balance the truths that God gives all things richly to enjoy and that we are to store up treasures in heaven. We wanted a space that would give us room to pour into our kids' education, have family fun, host extended family, care for foster kids, and offer rooms to people needing a place to stay. I often say the house is the worst financial decision we ever made but the best decision for the spiritual growth and discipleship for our family. Jen is homeschooling our kids, so we were able to build our home around this priority and it has been a significant blessing. I realize that God can work through any set of circumstances, and that our ways are not his ways, but I believe that he had this for us. The building process cost more than expected and took longer than expected (big surprises, I know), but God was faithful through all of it, and we saw him work in many ways. We finally moved into our home in 2020 just before Covid shut down Illinois.

Jen and I do not have concrete plans for the next 20 years, but I am intentionally looking to build into our kids and others that God allows us to be in relationship with. Hopefully this involves visiting national parks and enjoying God's amazing creation while being involved serving vulnerable members of our community. I do not desire a traditional retirement but to prioritize more time for family activities including ministry and service. I enjoy working with people and having discussions about generosity and contentment and plan to do that for as long as I am able. I also hope to help others in our company embrace leadership responsibilities. I believe it is possible to balance being actively involved with running a business while also having time for family and ministry. I am personally looking to grow in being generous with time, hospitality, and serving others. We live in a hurting world, and I want to shine the light of Christ in our community and greater Chicagoland.

The goal of our financial planning business is not profit or business value maximization but rather the long-term impact we will have on clients and their families. Ruth sold the business to me in the Spring of 2007 at a reasonable price because she desired to see it succeed over the long term and I had helped build the business. I used the same approach when Mike bought into the business a few years ago and hope to do the same in the future. The goal of this approach is that everyone would experience contentment and the joy of generosity.

Mike's Application

Has this book given you a lot to think about and challenged how you think about money? Me too! Even as a financial planner who spends a lot of time thinking about money, there will always be room for growth as we apply God's word to our lives. As we mentioned many times throughout the book, it is a process to properly align your use of money and to make financial changes that stick.

I like to think of finances like exercise. We all know that the true path to physical results is through a consistent diet and exercise plan. Sticking to a fad diet for a few days or having an extremely intense day at the gym every few weeks isn't going to produce the results you want. Neither is sticking to a stringent budget during the week only to splurge on the weekend going to change your finances. My hope is that this book has been a little bit like a personal trainer—giving you some knowledge and instruction to help you on the path of being purposeful with your finances.

To that end, I wanted to share how I think about a few issues from the Getting Practical chapters to illustrate intentional financial decisions in your mid-30s with a family. This is not a set of instructions—personal situations and convictions will always vary—but hopefully helpful insights into the thought process behind financial choices.

Cash Flow – With four young children, there is an additional facet to the normal cash flow decisions of how much to live off, give, and save. There is a seemingly endless number of things that we could be spending money on—clubs, teams, clothing, equipment, and on and on. Everyone wants the best for their children, and it can be tempting to think that the more we spend on them the better opportunities they will have and the greater the chance they grow up to be the people we desire them to be. One of my favorite quotes on this dilemma is from Abigail Van Buren who said, "If you want your children to turn out well, spend twice as much time with them, and half as much money."[1] My wife, Whitney, and I have tried to follow this advice to spend as much time with our children as we can. The money that we do spend (other than the necessities) is often geared at improving the time we have together. We've made significant investments to our backyard—not just so that we have memories (no doubt they will remember the first time they beat dad in basketball or mom and dad in pickleball. . . . On second thought, these things may never happen, but they will have memories of trying!) but also so that our home is a destination for their friends and we can have greater influence in those relationships. We have also made the decision to send our children to a private Christian school. This is no small cost, but we do view it as an investment in our children and we try to keep that perspective, which admittedly can be difficult when writing the tuition checks. These investments work, in part, because they align with how we understand the purpose of money.

Work, Saving, and Retirement – Although I do enjoy my job, I used to think that early retirement was the goal. I grew up with the FIRE movement (Financially Independent, Retire Early) and, while I never took my personal finances to that extreme, an early retirement seemed like an obvious goal to have. Over the years that goal has shifted as I learned and experienced more—both from working with clients and growing in my understanding of Scripture. Since I am not trying to aggressively save for an early retirement, cash flow is freed up to make some of the investments discussed above. This does not mean I have been putting off saving. I am still saving and following the advice Eric and I generally give, it just happens to be focused less on retirement and more on flexibility. I have seen the impact flexibility offers in many clients and that has created a desire in me to have that flexibility available if necessary.

Giving – Despite it being last in this list, giving is not the last thing we spend money on in our house. When we were younger, it was challenging to find a good balance between our incomes, cost of living, and our desire to be generous. I had always heard how important it was to begin giving early, when your income was smaller, because it would never get easier to give even as your income grows. With this in mind, several years ago we decided that we would commit to giving a certain percentage of income no matter how our income increases. While I am hesitant to use or recommend hard percentages out of concern of taking out the intentionality and joy of giving, this has worked well for us.

Final Thoughts

Our desire is for the body of Christ to handle their finances differently than the world does—to move beyond the default money moves and towards a purpose that aligns with your belief about God. We have enjoyed writing this book and hope it has been helpful to you and your family as you plan for the future while focusing on generosity and contentment in the present.

Citations

Chapter 1

   1. Erik Raymond, Chasing Contentment (Wheaton: Crossway, 2017).

Chapter 2

   1. The saying likely originates from Robert Quillen

Chapter 3

   1. Luke 12:6-21 ESV

   2. Arthur A. Just, Luke, InterVarsity Press, 2003, p. 208

Chapter 4

   1. Escape from Reason by Francis A. Schaeffer

   2. As counted by Howard Dayton

   3. What is Biblical Stewardship? https://www.ligonier.org/blog/what-biblical-stewardship/ 6/28/2019

   4. Bible.org Our Daily Bread 2/2/09

   5. Gospel and Kingdom by Graeme Goldsworthy

Chapter 5

   1. Nevertheless: The incredible story of one man's mission to change thousands of people's lives by John Kirby

   2. Dr. Martin Luther King, Jr.'s October 26,1967 speech at the Barratt Junior High School in Philadelphia, PA

   3. ABC World News with Diane Sawyer, June 7, 2010

   4. John Calvin, Institutes of the Christian Religion

5. https://pratyushbuddiga.substack.com/p/on-cards-crypto-and-christ?s=r

Chapter 6

1. C.S. Lewis, Mere Christianity
2. Jim Johnston, "Joyless Christianity is Dangerous", DesiringGod.org, October 21, 2015
3. What are the Odds? The Generosity Story of Janice Worth by Sheila Dolinger, January 1, 2020

Chapter 7

1. CXO Advisory Group studied over 6,500 predictions from 68 different professional investors who made public predictions between 1998 and 2012. The average accuracy of the prediction was 47%. In a similar study, Morgan Housel looked at the average S&P500 forecast from 22 chief market strategists of the biggest banks and brokerage firms from 2000-2014 and found that, on average, the annual forecasts missed the actual market performance by 14.6%.
2. Harsh Lessons in Modern Con Art by Mitch Anthony, December 1, 2017
3. We assume you have already come to the conclusion that the risk to investing in stocks and bonds is worth taking as well as Biblical. If you are unsure, we recommend starting with a short article "7 Biblical Principles for Saving and Investing Your Money" by Chris Cagle. For a more detailed review we recommend Money, Possessions, and Eternity by Randy Alcorn.

4. The Psychology of Money by Morgan Housel
5. Mutual Fund Landscape 2020 – Dimensional Fund Advisors
6. https://www.investopedia.com/investing/costs-investing/#:~:text=Active%20and%20passive%20funds%20carry,mutual%20funds%20averaged%20just%20 0.15%25.
7. https://www.investor.gov/financial-tools-calculators/calculators/compound-interest-calculator
8. S&P500 return annualized from 1926 through 2021, Dimensional Fund Advisors 2022 Matrix Book
9. 1-Month Treasury Bills return annualized from 1926 through 2019, Dimensional Fund Advisors 2020 Matrix Book
10. Berkshire Hathaway Annual Shareholder Meeting 2020

Chapter 8
1. World War II: The Economic Anomaly, A Wealth of Common Sense, October 10, 2019

Chapter 9
1. Howard Dayton, Building Your Finances God's Way
2. Epictetus, Discourses: With the Enchiridion and Fragments
3. Ron Blue, Splitting Heirs
4. Billhigh.com/legacy/a-good-man-leaves-an-inheritance-to-his-childrens-children/
   And Randy Alcorn Money, Possessions, and Eternity
5. Matthew 6:19-20

Conclusion

1. Abigail Van Buren, The Minister's Manual for 1993

For Further Reading

Introduction / Chapter 1

Chasing Contentment by Erik Raymond

Contentment, Prosperity, and God's Glory
by Jeremiah Burroughs

The Rare Jewel of Christian Contentment
by Jeremiah Burroughs

The Bruised Reed by Richard Sibbes

The Mortification of Sin by John Owen

George Whitfield by Arnold A. Dallimore

Becoming Dallas Willard by Gary Moon

Building Below the Waterline by Gordon MacDonald

Chapter 4

Money, Possessions, and Eternity by Randy Alcorn

Chapter 5

Every Good Endeavor by Timothy Keller

Chapter 6

Giving Is the Good Life by Randy Alcorn

Redeeming Money by Paul Tripp

Gospel Patrons by John Rinehart

Master Your Money by Ron Blue

Chapter 7

The Psychology of Money by Morgan Housel

Chapter 8

Retiring Well by John Dunlop

Chapter 9

Don't Waste Your Life by John Piper

The Duties of Parents by JC Ryle

Entrusted With a Child's Heart by Betsy Corning

Family Revision by Jeremy Pryor

Splitting Heirs by Ron Blue

About the Authors

MICHAEL MCKEVITT IS a partner at Guillaume & Freckman, Inc., a wealth management firm in the Chicago suburbs. He has worked there since his graduation from Taylor University in 2008. He is a CERTIFIED FINANCIAL PLANNER™ Professional, a Certified Kingdom Advisor®, and a Retirement Income Certified Professional®. He serves on the boards of several non-profits and is an active member at his church. Michael and his wife, Whitney, live in Wheaton, IL, and have four children.

ERIC FRECKMAN IS the managing partner of Guillaume & Freckman, Inc. Eric has been a financial planner since his graduation from Taylor University in 2000. He is a CERTIFIED FINANCIAL PLANNER™ Professional and a Certified Kingdom Advisor®. Eric and his wife, Jen, live in Inverness, IL, with their four children. They are active in their church, serving in small groups, youth ministry, and foster care.

Michael and Eric created the Purposeful Wealth Experience® to guide their client's understanding of the purpose for their finances and to help them manage their wealth responsibly. Find out more about them and this process at www.GF-Wealth.com.